ORTHO® ALL ABOUT

Roses

Written by Dr. Tommy Cairns

Meredith® Books
Des Moines, Iowa

Ortho All About Roses
Editor: Michael McKinley
Contributing Writer: Dr. Tommy Cairns
Contributing Technical Editor: Steve Jones
Contributing Photographer: Doug Hetherington
Copy Chief: Terri Frederickson
Publishing Operations Manager: Karen Schirm
Senior Editor, Asset and Information Manager: Phillip Morgan
Edit and Design Production Coordinator: Mary Lee Gavin
Editorial and Design Assistant: Kathleen Stevens
Book Production Managers: Pam Kvitne, Marjorie J. Schenkelberg,
    Rick von Holdt, Mark Weaver
Contributing Copy Editor: Nancy T. Engel
Contributing Proofreaders: Fran Gardner, Susan Lang, Stephanie Petersen
Other Contributors: Janet Anderson, Susan K. Ferguson

**Additional Editorial and Design Contributions
    from Art Rep Services**
Director: Chip Nadeau
Designer: LK Design

Meredith® Books
Executive Director, Editorial: Gregory H. Kayko
Executive Director, Design: Matt Strelecki
Managing Editor: Amy Tincher-Durik
Executive Editor: Benjamin W. Allen
Senior Associate Design Director: Tom Wegner
Marketing Product Manager: Brent Wiersma

Publisher and Editor in Chief: James D. Blume
Editorial Director: Linda Raglan Cunningham
Executive Director, New Business Development: Todd M. Davis
Executive Director, Sales: Ken Zagor
Director, Operations: George A. Susral
Director, Production: Douglas M. Johnston
Director, Marketing: Amy Nichols
Business Director: Jim Leonard

Vice President and General Manager: Douglas J. Guendel

Meredith Publishing Group
President: Jack Griffin
Senior Vice President: Karla Jeffries

Meredith Corporation
Chairman of the Board: William T. Kerr
President and Chief Executive Officer: Stephen M. Lacy

In Memoriam: E. T. Meredith III (1933–2003)

Photographers:
American Rose Society: 122
David Austin Roses: 115TL
Richard Baer: 21L, 68BL, 69CR, 71BR, 72TR, 73TC, 77TL,
    77TC, 81BC, 82TL, 82BL, 84TL, 86CR, 88TR, 89BR, 90BR,
    92TC, 93BL, 95TR, 97BL, 97TR, 97CR, 99BL, 102BC,
    104TL, 106CL, 106CR, 113BL, 114BR, 115CL, 115BR,
    116TL, 117TL, 117TC, 119CL, 119TC, 119BC, 120TL,
    120CR, 121CL, 121BL
Steve Brubaker/Rosefile.com: 69TL
David Cavagnaro/Garden Picture Library: 104BR
Conard-Pyle/Star Roses: 72CR, 87TR, 117BC
R. Todd Davis: 106R
Alan and Linda Detrick: 103TC
John Elsley: 101CL, 102BL, 104BC, 108TR, 112BR, 116BL,
    117BL
John Glover/Positive Images: 23L, 62
Greenheart/Nor'East Roses: 90TL, 90BL, 92BL, 94TL, 95BC,
    97TL, 97TC, 98BL
Saxon Holt: 36, 101BR, 102CR, 109TR, 109BR, 111TC
Irene Jeruss/Positive Images: 63
Andrew Lawson/The Garden Collection: 110BR
Janet Loughrey: 115TR
Susan McKessar/JustOurPictures.com: 86TR, 105TL
Jerry Pavia: 22T, 22B, 72TL, 89CL, 103BC, 109BC
Ann Reilly/Positive Images: 79TL
Howard Rice/Garden Picture Library: 27
Gene Sasse © courtesy of Weeks Roses: 120BR
Richard Shiell: 23R, 75BR, 76TC, 77TR, 77BR, 81TL, 87TL,
    88BL, 89TL, 100BC, 103BR, 104BL, 108BC
Robbie Tucker/Rosemania.com: 92TR
Laurie Zawiskie: 96TC

Cover: Glowing Peace, photograph by Doug Hetherington

Thanks to: Descanso Gardens, LaCanada Flintridge, CA; Dr.
John T. Dickman; Heirloom Rose Gardens, Saint Paul, OR;
Tony Liberta; Portland International Rose Test Gardens at
Washington Park; Rose Hills Company, Whittier, CA; The
Huntington Library, San Merino, CA; The Rose Garden at
Greenwood Park, Des Moines, IA.

All of us at Meredith® Books are dedicated to providing
you with the information and ideas you need to enhance
your home and garden. We welcome your comments and
suggestions about this book. Write to us at:
    Meredith Corporation
    Meredith Gardening Books
    1716 Locust St.
    Des Moines, IA 50309-3023

If you would like more information on other Ortho
products, call 800/225-2883 or visit us at: www.ortho.com

Note to the Readers: Due to differing conditions, tools,
and individual skills, Meredith Corporation assumes no
responsibility for any damages, injuries suffered, or losses
incurred as a result of following the information published
in this book. Before beginning any project, review the
instructions carefully, and if any doubts or questions
remain, consult local experts or authorities. Because codes
and regulations vary greatly, you always should check
with authorities to ensure that your project complies
with all applicable local codes and regulations. Always
read and observe all of the safety precautions provided by
manufacturers of any tools, equipment, or supplies, and
follow all accepted safety procedures.

CONTENTS

THE WIDE WORLD OF ROSES

By any other name, of course, this blossom would smell as sweet. But no matter what the century or culture, people have always celebrated the rose. From ancient times to today, in poetry and song, during wars and festivities, people from all walks of life have honored this "Queen of Flowers." In recognition of the rich history and versatility of this beloved blossom, the United States Congress has selected the rose as the national floral emblem of the United States. Roses are available in so many plant, flower, and color choices that almost every garden has a place for at least one, proving that successful rose growing is within everyone's reach.

Because roses are available in so many forms, few plants rival them in the home landscape. From the sweetest miniature rose potted in a container to the most profuse rambler cascading along a fence, from the fragrant charm of an old-fashioned garden rose to the stately elegance of a hybrid tea, there is a rose to suit every garden and gardener.

Roses provide structure and proportion to the landscape. They come in nearly every shape, size, and color imaginable. And with today's long-lasting repeat bloomers, roses are among the showiest and hardest working of all garden plants. Whether your gardening style is casual and relaxed or tailored and formal, roses are a welcome addition.

◀ **A simple, casually arranged collection of English roses and old garden roses illustrates the ease of blending color and form into a masterpiece for the indoors: Golden Celebration (cupped yellow), Evelyn (flat, creamy apricot), 'Baronne Prevost' (quartered, medium pink), and 'Salet' (light pink).**

Indoor-outdoor appeal

Roses cut fresh from the garden and brought into the house are a lovely reward. Filling a vase with roses is easy, and the results are spectacular. A collection of pastel English roses and old garden roses can create a wonderfully serene arrangement, and the bright colors of many hybrid teas add vibrancy to a room. And sweet-scented blooms are, of course, an added bonus.

Many serious rose growers are eager to experiment with new varieties. Their enthusiasm can be contagious, and casual gardeners—or even novices with limited space—can translate that experience into stunning results for their own gardens. A flush of antique roses scrambling over a fence, wall, or trellis is a breathtaking sight, and a few miniature roses spilling from pots on a terrace are a charming addition of color and dimension.

There's no limit to the number of ways you can grow and display roses.

▷ **Formal rose gardens employ low-growing hedges such as boxwood to define precise boundaries.**

▽ **A profusion of old and modern roses combine with perennials such as pinks, iris, and foxglove to give this cottage garden delightful exuberance.**

In the pages that follow, you will discover practical suggestions for incorporating roses into your landscape. You will also find easy, step-by-step growing instructions, plus a gallery of more than 350 recommended varieties. The most popular of all flowers is unfortunately often misused and misunderstood. Choosing the right roses is half the battle; the other is caring for them intelligently. Take advantage of the versatility of roses, and you will enjoy their delightful gifts for years to come.

ANATOMY OF THE ROSE

Roses are classified by the form and color of their flowers, as well as their seed structures, leaves, and stems. It's useful to be familiar with this anatomy because plant descriptions refer to them.

Flowers

This structure is technically known as the **corolla.** The corolla is made up of **petals,** with the number determining whether the rose is classified as single, semidouble, double, full, or very full.

A quartered flower is one with petals that open in such a way that, when viewed from above, the rose appears to be divided into quadrants.

A solitary bloom appears at the top of the flower stem of some roses; these are usually referred to as one-to-a-stem roses. When multiple flowers appear on a stem, the grouping is known as a spray or a cluster.

Flowers open from flower buds, which are initially covered by leaflike green sheaths known as **sepals.** Collectively, the sepals and the bulbous structure below them—the **calyx tube**—are known as the **calyx.** As a flower opens, the sepals turn down and may eventually be hidden by the flower. Some sepals are small and plain; others are large and frilled.

When a flower has fully opened, thin filaments called **stamens** become visible in the center of the flower, which is called the **disk.** Stamens, the male reproductive portion of the flower, release **pollen** from parts at their tips called **anthers.** The stamens of roses are usually yellow, although sometimes they are red or

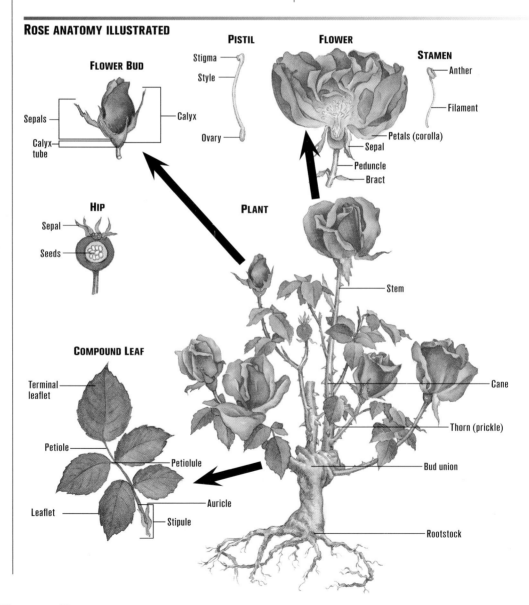

ROSE ANATOMY ILLUSTRATED

FLOWER BUD — Sepals, Calyx, Calyx tube

PISTIL — Stigma, Style, Ovary

FLOWER — Petals (corolla), Sepal, Peduncle, Bract

STAMEN — Anther, Filament

HIP — Sepal, Seeds

PLANT — Stem, Cane, Thorn (prickle), Bud union, Rootstock

COMPOUND LEAF — Terminal leaflet, Petiole, Petiolule, Leaflet, Auricle, Stipule maroon. The female portion of the flower, the **pistil**, is located at the center of the stamens. Only its topmost portion, the **stigma**, can be seen; hidden below it is the **style**, a slender tube that leads to the **ovary**, where seeds form if fertilization takes place. Seeds develop from ovules, egglike objects that are borne on structures called carpels within the ovary.

Once a rose has been pollinated—either by its own pollen or by pollen from another rose—the ovary swells and a seed-bearing fruit called the **hip** forms after the flowers fade. The hips of some roses are bright red or orange, with a characteristic pear, oval, or urn shape. Experts can often identify the variety of a rose by its distinctive hips alone.

Canes and stems

The main branches of rose bushes are known as **canes**. These arise from the **crown**, the point where the branches are joined to the **root shank**. On roses that have been budded (grafted) to more vigorous root systems, the point where the canes are grafted to the roots is called the **bud union**; the bud union functions as the crown. A new cane that arises from the crown or the bud union is often called a **basal break**.

Stems are growths emanating from the canes and terminating in flowers. Stem length depends on the class of rose. For example, most hybrid teas have longer stems, making them good for cut flowers.

Both the canes and the stems are usually covered by red or green **thorns** (also known as **prickles**), although some roses are thornless. Thorns vary in size, shape, and number. They can be so distinctive that they alone can be used to identify certain roses.

Leaves

Roses have **compound leaves**, which are made up of several **leaflets**. Most modern roses have five-leaflet leaves except in the area near the flower, where three-leaflet leaves usually appear instead. Old garden roses may have seven, nine, or even more leaflets. The top leaflet, called the **terminal leaflet**, is attached to the rest by a small stem known as a **petiole**; the other leaflets have stalks known as **petiolules**. The leaf's base has a winglike appendage known as the **stipule**; the tip of the stipule is called the **auricle**.

New stem growth emanates from a bud eye in the **leaf axil**, the point at which a leaf joins the stem. The part of the stem between the highest leaf and the flower is known as the **peduncle**, also referred to as the neck. Peduncles are generally thornless and soft wooded, and vary in length and thickness depending on the rose variety. Often, a small leaflike structure known as a **bract** appears partway down the peduncle.

WHAT'S IN A NAME: ROSE NOMENCLATURE

Botanical names: Some roses are botanical species—a group of plants with similar inherited characteristics found growing naturally in the wild. An example is *Rosa rugosa*, a hardy species native to the Far East. Botanical species are always expressed scientifically with at least two parts to each name, always in italicized Latin. The first indicates the genus. All roses are members of the genus *Rosa*. The second indicates the species. *Rosa rugosa* is a group, or species, of roses sharing unique characteristics passed on from generation to generation that set that group apart from other species.

Sometimes there is a subsidiary group (a botanical variety) that occurs naturally within a species and is expressed as a roman name in parentheses. For example, *Rosa rugosa alba* is a naturally occurring white-flowered variety of the cerise-flowered species *Rosa rugosa*.

Horticultural and commercial names: Most roses in cultivation are the product of careful breeding and selection. When rose breeders are ready to introduce a new cultivated variety (called a cultivar), they must register the new plant's official name—which must be unique to that plant—with the International Registration Authority for Roses. A cultivar name is capitalized, printed in regular typeface (never italic), and enclosed by single quotation marks. Once registered, it is the official name of that cultivar worldwide. A cultivar name must be universally available and can never be trademarked.

In 1958 rose breeders began coding cultivar names with the first three letters of the breeder's name or the company's name in capital letters, to which they added lowercase letters. In 1978 this coding became official practice.

The fancy name previously used for the cultivar name was now often trademarked as a commercial name. For example, in 1961 David Austin introduced his first English rose, trademarked its fancy name Constance Spry, and registered its cultivar name as 'AUSfirst'.

In this book, initial-capped names not enclosed in single quotation marks are the fancy names used commercially; most are trademarked or registered. Only official cultivar names appear in single quotation marks.

FLOWERS OF ALL SHAPES AND SIZES (AND FRUITS TOO)

Choices of size and form

All roses are not created equal. There is great variation in blossom size, shape, color combinations, number of petals, and fragrance. Bloom sizes range in diameter from 5 to 6 inches down to ½ inch. The number of petals is a measure of the fullness of a flower. Roses range from the simplest four-petaled blossom to the fullest flowers of 100 petals or more. Petals, in turn, have their own structure: plain, reflexed, ruffled, or frilled like a carnation. The overall shape of the blossom comes in an equally diverse selection—globular, open cupped, quartered, flat, rosette, pompon, and high centered (often called exhibition form). For all blossom types, petal substance—a measure of petal durability—is an important criterion for selecting and judging roses. Petals with substance are tough. They feel thicker than more delicate petals—almost leathery. These blossoms last longer and can better sustain exposure to high temperatures.

Bloom form

Rose blossoms have diverse shapes from broad, flat simplicity to high-centered sculptural elegance. Single-petaled varieties have a natural, "wild" charm, with flat, wide-open blooms and a central boss, or cluster, of stamens. The form of a many-petaled rose changes as it opens, usually exposing the central stamens. The blooms of some modern shrub roses and old garden roses are shaped like globes and rosettes, or organized in quarters. The hybrid tea shape is characterized by a high, pointed center and symmetrically unfurling petals.

Petal count

The number of petals is a measure of the fullness of a flower. With roses, various terms are used to describe the petal count: single flowers (4 to 8 petals), semidouble (9 to 16 petals), double (17 to 25 petals), full (26 to 40 petals), and very full (41 to more than 100 petals).

The bonus of rose hips

Some roses that only flower once in the spring put on an autumn display of attractive fruit called hips. Most shrub roses and old garden roses produce massive clusters of rose hips of various shapes and sizes—round, elongated, even prickly. For instance, 'Frau Dagmar Hartopp' has some of the largest tomatolike red hips. An interesting display of hips extends the pleasure of roses well into fall and winter.

Fragrance

Don't forget fragrance when selecting a new rose; many possess a perfume that will fill a room or even a garden. Scents range from those resembling cloves or citrus to green apples, and from sweet honey to sharp spice.

Signature
High centered
Hybrid tea

Playboy
Single
Floribunda

Golden Celebration
Cupped
Shrub

Blueberry Hill
Semidouble
Floribunda

Evelyn
Flat open
Shrub

'Madame Hardy'
Quartered with
central pip
Old garden rose

'Salet'
Quartered pompon
Old garden rose

'Aunt Gerry'
Fully opened
Hybrid tea

Bloom size

Generally the largest blooms (3 to 6 inches across) are seen on hybrid teas, grandifloras, old garden roses, shrubs, and some climbers. Intermediate-size flowers (2 to 3 inches in diameter) are found on floribundas, but their characteristic of producing sprays or clusters makes the bloom mass on a single stem appear spectacular. The next smaller bloom size (1 to 2 inches across) is that of the minifloras, followed by miniatures (½ to 1 inch across).

▲ Hybrid tea
(Diana, Princess
of Wales)

▲ Old garden rose,
Portland ('Rose de Rescht')

◄ Shrub
(DayDream)

▲ Floribunda
(Judy Garland)

◄ Miniflora
(Double Gold)

▲ Miniature
(Dancing Flame)

▲ Hips
(*Rosa rugosa*)

Flowers and fruits on this page are shown actual size.

FLOWERS OF NEARLY EVERY COLOR

ROSE COLOR PATTERNS

▲ Solid color (Julia Child)

▲ Bicolor ('Duet')

▲ Striped (Scentimental)

▲ Multicolor (Rainbow's End)

▲ Blended (Double Delight)

▲ Handpainted (Brilliant Pink Iceberg)

The astonishing range of colors offered by modern roses is unmatched by any other kind of flower. Except for true blue and true black, there is a rose available in nearly every hue and shade—and breeders are working hard on both blue and black as well. New varieties in the mauve range have been steadily pushing roses toward the blue side of the color spectrum, and advances in genetic engineering promise a true blue rose in the near future.

The American Rose Society, custodian of rose registrations, has developed the system of official color classifications used in this book. Examples of each color classification are shown on the facing page. Subtle variations within each color classification result in a nearly infinite variety of color selections in this remarkable genus.

Flower color patterns

Increasing the color choices are a range of color patterns in each color classification, including **solid color** (single uniform color), **bicolor** (upper surface and underside of petals are different colors), **multicolor** (flowers turn different colors as they age, resulting in flowers of different colors on the same plant at the same time), **blended** (one color merges into another toward the petal edge), **striped** (different colors in sharply defined streaks and blotches), and **handpainted** (different colors in softly defined "watercolor" streaks and blushes).

DON'T FORGET THE FOLIAGE

▲ Dark green, glossy, large (Sheila's Perfume)

▲ Light green, matte, small ('Pink Grootendorst')

▲ Burgundy new foliage (Europeana)

▲ Gray, matte, small (Rosa glauca)

Rose foliage is an often overlooked yet important ornamental feature, as it appears long before the first blossom and remains prominent throughout the growing season. Leaves can have a glossy, semiglossy, or matte finish in a range of colors from light green to dark green, even bronze tinted and gray-green.

All these factors contribute to a versatile plant. Some roses, in fact, are grown more for their outstanding ornamental foliage than for their flowers. *Rosa glauca*, for example, is a species rose with small pink flowers that appear once in late spring. Its silvery gray foliage, however, is elegant throughout the growing season and considered by plant connoisseurs to be a staple in the silver garden.

In general, glossy, leathery foliage is more resistant to attack by a fungal disease such as powdery mildew because the waxy coating provides a barrier.

AMERICAN ROSE SOCIETY COLOR CLASSIFICATIONS AND THEIR ABBREVIATIONS

▲ **White, w**
(Iceberg)

▲ **Apricot blend, ab**
(Valencia)

▲ **Near white, w**
(Sheer Bliss)

▲ **White blend, w**
(Moonstone)

▲ **Light pink, lp**
(Royal Highness)

▲ **Light yellow, ly**
(Elina)

▲ **Apricot, ab**
(Marilyn Monroe)

▲ **Orange-pink blend, op** (Abraham Darby)

▲ **Pink blend, pb**
(Gemini)

▲ **Medium pink, mp**
(Queen Elizabeth)

▲ **Medium yellow, my**
(Behold)

▲ **Orange blend, ob**
(Chris Evert)

▲ **Orange pink, op**
(Sheer Elegance)

▲ **Red blend, rb**
(Betty Boop)

▲ **Deep pink, dp**
(Apothecary's Rose)

▲ **Yellow blend, yb**
(Glowing Peace)

▲ **Orange, ob**
(Livin' Easy)

▲ **Orange-red blend, or (This Is The Day)**

▲ **Medium red, mr**
(Olympiad)

▲ **Mauve blend, m**
(Neptune)

▲ **Deep yellow, dy**
(Midas Touch)

▲ **Russet, r**
(Hot Cocoa)

▲ **Orange red, or**
(Trumpeter)

▲ **Dark red, dr**
(Black Magic)

▲ **Mauve, m**
(Ebb Tide)

PLANTS COME IN ALL SIZES AND SHAPES

When selecting roses for your garden, remember that the architectural shape and ultimate dimensions are important. They give form to the landscape and proportion to its elements. Fortunately, you can grow roses almost anywhere that gets at least six hours of sun a day. Grow them as flowering shrubs, in mixed beds and borders, among herbs in containers, underplanted with annuals, surrounding a mailbox or light post, screening a fence, scrambling up trees, trailing over arches or arbors, or cascading down a bank or over a stone wall. The key is to ensure that each variety you choose is suitable for the use you have in mind.

Environmental factors and personal preference aren't the only considerations that influence selection. How a rose is used in the landscape—as an accent, a hedge, or a backdrop in a border—also determines which one is best. If you intend to train the rose up a wall or along a fence, for example, then climbing roses or ramblers are best. For a mass planting, hybrid teas and grandifloras are dramatic, but they work less well by themselves as single specimens. The flowers are quite spectacular, but their sometimes leggy form can be unattractive. A shrubbier rose

is a better choice as a single plant in an existing landscape. Shrub roses have a rounded form that works as a blooming hedge.

If your garden provides the necessary sunlight and soil conditions—and if you take a little time to explore your home landscape—you can easily pick the rose that's right for you. Check out the illustrations and brief descriptions on these pages for roses that will thrive in your yard. Most of the forms shown here are genetic, or naturally occuring; a few— notably the patio tree and the standard tree—are grafted forms.

A. Patio Tree: A great way to grow floribundas and miniatures about 4 feet off the ground, the patio tree is also excellent in pots. An exposed plant may be susceptible to winter damage.

B. Miniature: This dense, low-growing rose covers itself with tiny blooms, usually in clusters. Use it for edging, growing in pots, or rockeries. Plants reach 18 to 24 inches tall.

C. Floribunda: Known for large clusters of medium-size blooms that cover the bush all season long, the plant is generally hardy and easy to maintain. It usually grows to about 3 feet tall.

D. Hybrid Tea: This premier cut flower is easily recognized by one single, sculptural, high-centered bloom per long stem. The flowers are usually large and symmetrical. Plants can grow to about 5 feet tall.

E. Climber: Actually a shrub with long, arching stems, this rose grows 6 to 20 feet tall when trained on a wall, trellis, or fence. Train the long canes in a horizontal position to promote bloom production.

F. Pillar: A smaller category of climbing roses, this type is often trained around a tall vertical support, covering itself with flowers at each lateral. It can reach heights between 6 to 10 feet tall.

G. Old Garden Roses: These pre-1867 types come in a range of sizes, shapes, and flower forms. They are often fragrant, and many bloom only once. Plants can grow 6 to 8 feet or higher.

H. Grandiflora: It is similar to the hybrid teas, but is identified by its unique ability to send up clusters of large hybrid tea-type blossoms on strong straight stems. Plants are normally 6 to 8 feet tall.

I. Modern shrub: Recent hybridizing breakthroughs combine the old garden rose flower form and fragrance with modern colors and recurrent blooms. Plants reach 3 to 7 feet tall.

J. Groundcover: Plants in this landscaping category of vigorous, disease-resistant low growers spread up to 8 feet wide and are used for bedding and massing. Varieties are usually hardy.

K. Standard Tree: It offers an excellent way to grow hybrid teas and floribundas about 6 feet off the ground, often for a formal effect. Plants are subject to winter damage in northern areas if left unprotected.

L. Rambler: Given adequate space, this type of rose will grow 30 feet tall and wide to cover a tree or even a house. Most have only one bloom cycle each year. Plants tend to be winter hardy.

ADDING BEAUTY TO THE LANDSCAPE WITH ROSES

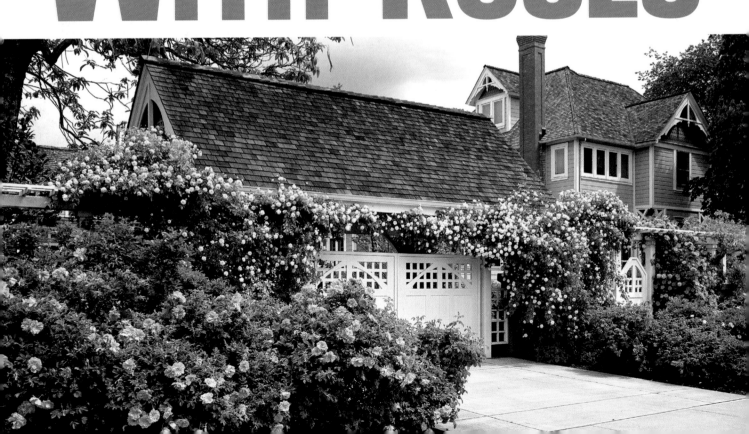

Because of their dynamic range in color, size, shape, and growth habit, roses lend themselves to many garden situations. Before choosing roses varieties for your garden, take a moment to evaluate your landscaping requirements. These simple guidelines will help you figure out where and how to start:

▓ Decide on the role you want the rose to perform in the space you have allotted, whether it's to produce flowers for indoor arrangements, form a showy border, erect an impenetrable hedge or privacy screen, cover a wall or trellis, create spots of color in containers on a terrace, or deliver fragrance near the patio.

▓ Start small and allow for later expansion as you succeed and gain confidence. But beware of the "vanishing lawn syndrome"— your devotion to roses may turn into an addiction as you slowly carve out more space!

▓ Select a garden style—from casual country-cottage look to extremely formal—that pleases you. Keep in mind the surrounding plants and landscape as you make these decisions.

▓ Decide on the exact location—whether it fits into an existing garden or starts a whole new one. Make sure the location can support your dream roses with plenty of sun (at least six hours daily), fertile soil, and adequate drainage.

▓ Develop a simple plan and allow the practice of garden making to inspire your evolving tastes and needs. Sketch out your ideas on paper and try to estimate costs.

▓ Finally, peruse the "Gallery of Roses" starting on page 64 to find the roses that are sure to succeed in your setting.

▲ **Because they often have a leggy, upright form with flowers atop long stems, hybrid tea roses may be thought of as plants for formal gardens. Here, however, an informal bed of them presents a spectacular show.**

▼ **Floribunda, shrub, and polyantha roses combine with perennials to frame a casual, colorful entryway.**

◄ **Mary Rose grows along the sidewalk as New Dawn climbs over the garage and America graces the entrance of this Midwestern landscape.**

Add a sense of drama

A classic approach to growing roses in the home landscape is to create living barriers or walls of color. For instance, dress up that streetside fence with a stunning display of roses in front of it—floribundas, low groundcovers, or even a low-growing climber or shrub trained along the rails. Multiple plants of a single variety can provide a pleasing effect. Include fragrance as an extra gift to passersby. Try one of the Simplicity Series, available in white, red, purple, pink, and yellow—or the neon orange floribunda, Livin' Easy.

Add a finishing touch to perennial beds with a border of white miniatures or low-growing floribundas in front—or use them to adorn a pathway leading to the front door, a bed along the drive, or in masses along each side of your patio. An excellent choice is the popular white floribunda Iceberg, or the white miniature rose Gourmet Popcorn.

Create a solid bank of color with roses on a hillside or steep slope. They will be easier to maintain than lawn grass. For this purpose some groundcover roses are ideal—for instance, any of the Flower Carpet Series.

If your purpose for growing roses is to provide cut flowers for your home, concentrate on varieties with strong, straight stems and fragrant blossoms. Site them where harvesting will not disrupt your colorful garden display. Choose from the elegantly sculptured flowers of hybrid teas or the wide color range and informal flower forms of modern shrub roses.

ADDING HEIGHT WITH CLIMBERS

Perhaps the most dramatic way to use roses in the landscape is to employ climbers, pillars, and standards. They elevate blossoms to eye level and higher, creating a vertical display against which most perennials and annuals just can't compete. The effect is a romantic vision that adds accent and beauty to any garden. There are many ways to incorporate climbers into the garden, including on fences, walls, trellises, arbors, pergolas, and gazebos. If you have the space, you can even grow roses up the trunk of a tree.

Fences and walls

Consider converting that weather-beaten split-rail fence (or even an unsightly chain-link fence) into a curtain of color. Lush foliage can fill in the spaces, adding both a sense of depth and separation. The long canes produced by climbers can be woven neatly in and out of the structure as they grow. For the best results, plant one variety at regular 4- to 5-foot intervals and the intertwining canes will eventually produce a solid wall of beauty and fragrance. Grooming and training over several years will create a charming tapestry.

To cover a wall in the garden, train the canes into position using supports. On masonry walls, a series of eyebolts with wires arranged horizontally or in a fan shape can direct the canes. Or erect a trellis or lattice frame, and anchor the canes with horticultural tape. Add hinges, and the trellis can be removed for house painting and maintenance. 'New Dawn' and 'Zéphirine' Drouhin are both suited for training up walls.

▼ **Whether stretched out along a fence or trained against a wall, 'New Dawn' is one of the hardiest climbers, with aboveground growth hardy to at least Zone 5.**

▲ Eden, or Eden Climber (also known as Pierre de Ronsard), is an excellent climbing rose for pillars and posts. Here it is trained on a tuteur, or pyramid-shaped column of lattice.

Pillars and posts

A number of varieties perform wonderfully when trained to wrap around a pillar or post. This allows you the freedom to create columns of color arising from mixed beds and borders. True climbers are inappropriate for this purpose, as they are often too large and vigorous. Try the pillar-type varieties such as red 'Don Juan', yellow Golden Showers, or multicolored 'Joseph's Coat'. Or use a standard tree version of your favorite hybrid tea, floribunda, or miniature rose to create a vertical effect within a bed of annuals and perennials.

▲ 'Lavender Lassie' is a vigorous hybrid musk ideal for climbing over arbors and pergolas.

▲ 'Paul's Himalayan Musk Rambler' can grow to enormous heights of 40 feet or more and spill out of tall trees.

Arbors and pergolas

What more perfect way to highlight roses in a garden setting than with a rose-laden archway as an entrance? Plant two or more bushes of the same variety on either side of an arbor or arch and train their canes to go over the top and down the other side. This marriage of canes from both sides of the framework produces a magnificent display of roses all the way around it. The concept can be expanded using a pergola- or gazebo-type structure. A length of pathway can be lined and covered with a series of arbors that creates a virtual tunnel of roses in the garden. Imagine a walk down a rose-draped pathway, rich with the fragrance of 'Zéphirine Drouhin', and sunlight streaming through a skylight of soft pink roses.

Shout it from the rooftops

Some varieties of roses love to ramble on their own up into trees— even over the rooftops of houses. These so-called ramblers usually need little maintenance. If you have adequate space, try the pink climbing polyantha 'Mlle Cécile Brünner, Climbing', the soft pink 'Paul's Himalayan Musk Rambler,' or the yellow Lady Banks rose. Some ramblers, including the latter two, bloom only once—but abundantly— in spring.

MASSING: GROUNDCOVERS, BEDS, HEDGES, AND EDGING

For nonstop color and bloom on banks or in beds, roses can't be beat. Low-growing and wide-spreading varieties make excellent groundcovers; small rounded forms (especially miniature roses) are good for edging; and taller forms work well massed in large beds or as hedges.

Groundcovers

Groundcover roses are ideal for a massed planting. They bloom over a long period in a variety of colors that stand out against attractive green leaves. Varieties with bold-colored blooms can visually divide your lawn into separate areas. Or plant them in front of taller shrubs to heighten interest and help keep down weeds.

Many groundcover roses are so tough and versatile that in some areas they serve as freeway plantings. Use them to line paths and driveways with ribbons of color and to stabilize slopes and banks. Their spreading, shallow roots help prevent erosion while providing color.

Choose varieties with lush leaves and long, limp, narrow canes that can spread 4 to 8 feet. A single plant may eventually

▲ **Carpet of Color is a shrub rose with a compact, rounded form and disease-resistant foliage ideal for close planting in a bed. It provides nonstop color from late spring to fall.**

GOOD ROSES FOR BEDS

Amber Queen	Julia Child
Belle Story	Margaret Merril
Brass Band	Nicole
Chris Evert	Pat Austin
Crimson Bouquet	Rockin' Robin
Diana, Princess of	Sexy Rexy
Wales	Scentimental
French Lace	'The Fairy'
Gift of Life	What a Peach

GOOD ROSES FOR GROUNDCOVERS

Space these plants 2 feet apart; plan on them growing 2 to 3 feet tall.

Baby Boomer	Pillow Fight
Behold	Rainbow's End
Cupcake	Red Cascade
Flower Carpet	Red Ribbons
Gizmo	Bonica
Gourmet Popcorn	Starry Night
Harm Saville	White Meidiland
Magic Carrousel	Yellow Ribbons

▼ **Alba Meidiland is a very popular groundcover rose that can rapidly spread 6 to 10 feet wide. Many groundcover roses and climbers get their long, lax canes from *Rosa wichurana* in their breeding.**

cover 30 to 40 square feet with a height of only 1 to 2 feet. The clustered flowers of the best groundcover roses often last a long time and require no deadheading before each period of bloom. They work well in hard-to-reach garden spots because they require little care.

Beds

For a grand garden statement, fill an entire bed with many plants of one rose variety. Seen from a distance or from above, that bed will have tremendous visual impact.

The best rose varieties for bedding preserve their color as they age, keep flowering after the first flush of bloom, and have an appealing form or habit. Floribundas, modern shrubs, and miniatures bring continuous color throughout the season by providing plentiful clusters, or sprays, of flowers.

Research the mature height of the roses you want to grow. If you place your rose bed against a tall yew hedge or a wall, you may want to grow taller roses in the back. If you create an island bed, taller plants will likely be in the middle. The center is an attractive place for rose trees, surrounded by miniatures or floribundas.

When planting rose bushes in a bed allow room for air circulation and access around the plants for deadheading, grooming, and cutting. The planting distance between hybrid teas, miniatures, and floribundas is about 2 feet; the space between shrub or groundcover roses is about 3 feet. Mulching between roses will reduce weeds and maintain soil moisture.

Hedges

Because of their thicketlike character, most rose hedges tend to be informal. They have a spreading, arching nature and are not suited for small spaces. As a result they work

GOOD ROSES FOR HEDGES

Space these plants 2 to 2½ feet apart.

Betty Boop	Livin' Easy
Bonica	Purple Simplicity
Cherry Meidiland	Red Simplicity
Gizmo	Sevillana
'Grootendorst Red'	Simplicity
'Iceberg'	Sunsprite
Knock Out	White Simplicity

best in large country, cottage, or suburban gardens, where the severity of formal hedges is inappropriate. They are excellent choices when you want to create privacy screens or barriers, block out ugly views, or divide the garden into rooms—all with more color and interest than a formal hedge.

▶ Behold makes an outstanding edging rose. Its compact size and glossy, disease-resistant foliage allow for close planting. And its continuous bold yellow color is a lovely contrast to lighter yellow and apricot hybrid tea roses—providing interest while the hybrid teas rest between bloom cycles.

▽ A variety of shrub and old garden roses creates an exuberant informal hedge along this wrought-iron fence in Idaho. In the foreground the English roses Perdita and Belle Story are interplanted with Sally Holmes. The old garden rose 'Zephirine Drouhin' provides a deeper shade of pink in the background.

Informal rose hedges vary in height but tend to be between 3 and 6 feet tall. The best varieties for hedges are upright but branch well at the base to produce foliage and flowers clear to the ground. Hedges of shrub and floribunda roses look like thickets if you plant them close together (about 2 feet apart). Old garden roses and some shrub roses have a wide-spreading, arching form; they should be planted 4 feet apart.

Edging

Small roses are perfect for edging island beds, borders, foundations, and hardscape elements such as paths, patios, driveways, and steps. When they are planted close enough to visually connect, edging roses work very well at the front of a sunny bed or border, where they add a garland of color. They also effectively cover the bare canes of hybrid teas and other leggy shrubs.

Roses used for edging should be sturdy and compact. Miniature and miniflora roses in particular meet these requirements, and many flower all season. The best edging roses stand 18 to 24 inches tall. Look for compact size and color compatibility with neighboring plants.

GOOD ROSES FOR EDGING

Height is generally 1 to 2 feet. For edging, space the following varieties 18 to 24 inches apart.

Applause	Magic Carrousel
Baby Boomer	'Peaches 'N' Cream'
Behold	Picotee
Cupcake	Pillow Fight
Gizmo	Ralph Moore
Gourmet Popcorn	Rise 'N' Shine
Hot Tamale	Scentsational
Kristin	Sun Sprinkles

SMALL SPACES AND CONTAINERS

A small garden changes the focus of rose growing from wide swaths of color to the beauty of individual plants. Even when crowded by other plants, each rose stands alone when it comes to form and fragrance, because you experience it up close. Use flowers of similar color intensity in small spaces. Mixing strong and soft colors can be jarring.

ROSES FOR NARROW BEDS

Amber Queen
Double Gold
Gizmo
Jilly Jewel
Lemon Gems
Miss Flippins
Pillow Fight
Rockin' Robin
Scentsational
What a Peach

▲ **This narrow bed against a warm-toned stone wall makes the perfect home for a row of Amber Queen.**

Narrow beds

In narrow beds and limited space, 8- to 12-foot trellised climbers work well on the walls of your house. Unless your house is very tall, ramblers would be too vigorous and hard to control in a small space.

Roses can work as foundation plantings in a little garden where you can plant a row of billowing miniatures, small shrubs, or tall roses with a narrow, upright habit. Plant the roses away from the drip line of the roof, and make sure the eaves don't shade your roses or block them from rain.

Containers

Roses grown in containers bring season-long color and fragrance to decks, patios, and balconies. Potted roses also work well as focal points in formal gardens, as border accents, in sunny doorways, and alongside garden gates and paths. Although many roses grow well in containers, the best choices are those that stay narrow and upright or form dense floral mounds. Upright roses are suited to a close grouping. Round bushes need more space; they look good standing alone or in more widely spread groups. Miniature and miniflora roses are ideal for growing in containers; their small size and dense habit make them well-suited to smaller pots than are required for other kinds of roses.

Hanging and cascading effects

Some rose varieties have a natural tendency to spread and drape, making them perfect choices to grow behind a retaining wall. These varieties, with flexible canes drooping gracefully and flowering along the length of the cane, are also ideal for hanging baskets. Growing roses in a hanging basket gives them the advantage of excellent air circulation, which helps prevent fungal disease. Miniatures and some climbing varieties with fast repeat-bloom cycles that keep their display colorful throughout the growing season are most suitable for hanging baskets.

ROSES FOR CONTAINERS

Behold	Minnie Pearl
French Lace	Petite Perfection
Glowing Amber	Red Cascade
Hot Tamale	Sexy Rexy
Ingrid Bergman	Stainless Steel
Knock Out	Sun Flare
Lemon Gems	World War II Memorial
Party Girl	Rose

▶ **A collection of miniature roses provides a feeling of abundance in a confined area. With extra care, miniature roses can thrive in pots that are quite small.**

▶ **A rose spilling out of a hanging basket provides season-long color where space is in short supply. Shown here is 'Little White Lies,' a cascading miniature rose.**

Small climbers

Some small climbers, shrubs, and miniatures provide height and dense coverage, with flowers and foliage along the length of their stems for a full, lush appearance. Moreover, varieties that grow only 3 to 5 feet tall look well groomed and require little maintenance to control their width and height. Short climbers provide a blaze of color in an upright growth pattern

without invading nearby plants. This tidy behavior makes them ideal for small spaces. With grooming, some groundcover roses can also be trained to grow vertically in a tight area.

In containers small climbers can expand the intimate landscape of a deck, patio, or balcony into the vertical dimension. Cultivate them in decorative 15- to 20-gallon pots and tubs, and provide a simple

▶ **A number of tall miniatures with an upright form can be trained on supports as small climbers. Shown here is Little Charm.**

lattice to support the canes. The lattice should be rectangular and about 3 to 4 feet wide, or fan shape and about 5 feet wide at the top.

Standards and patio trees

Tree roses, or standards, are rose bushes raised off the ground by grafting them onto rose stock grown to several feet tall. Because the flowers are elevated, the form and color of the bush are easy to see. Tree roses have the top-heavy look of topiary. They make excellent focal points and can dominate the center of a bed or bring height and color to a border. Use them to flank a gate, a piece of sculpture, or the entrance to a path.

You can buy standards as 36-inch trees, 24-inch trees (patio trees), 18-inch trees (suited for miniature roses), and in some cases, 60- or 72-inch weeping trees. Short tree roses need no permanent support, although a support rod is advisable for the first few years. You may need an umbrella-shape support for large, weeping trees.

▶ **Standard roses flanking an entry make it look more important, framing it with color and whimsical form.**

INTEGRATING ROSES INTO MIXED BEDS AND BORDERS

➤ English roses mix with foxgloves and hardy geraniums in this predominantlly pink border. The pink rose in the foreground is Heritage.

▼ An all-white rose garden imparts a cool and formal effect.

It used to be that roses were relegated to their own corner of the garden. This Victorian attitude left nothing to show in the rose garden but canes and barren earth for most of the year. Thankfully, roses are now integrated with the rest of the garden, sharing space with garden plants of every size, shape, and texture. With their arching growth pattern, roses welcome companion plants growing through and around them. Roses, in fact, can grow and mix well nearly anywhere in the landscape.

Companion plants for roses

In your overall garden plan, any plant—whether it's an annual, perennial, bulb, shrub, herb, grass, vine, or small tree—can be combined with roses to dynamic effect. When selecting companion plants, consider color, shape, texture, and size, as well as how these elements will enhance or detract from your strategy. Companion plants can fill the spaces around roses while providing a continuous harmony of color throughout the year. They insert color between rose bloom cycles and provide structure to the landscape. For example, annuals are available in a multitude of hues to either contrast or harmonize with your

▲ This yellow-themed bed leans toward pink with apricot roses ('Buff Beauty') and warm pink and ivory ('Cornelia').

▲ The reds and oranges of Montezuma and Marmelade Skies add to the heat of this warm-toned bed of roses.

choice of roses. Perennials and vines extend the season of bloom and often provide an architectural element, as do ornamental grasses. Contrasting foliage plants and herbs can create a pleasing textural counterpoint in the rose garden.

The possibilities are endless and completely up to the individual. Find out what works for you and your garden. Choose familiar plants from a local nursery or garden center. In cooler areas, consider spring-flowering bulbs that are winter hardy. The most popular companion plant for roses is clematis, which twines and climbs throughout the rose's foliage, filling holes with bright, starry blossoms. And don't forget annuals such as pansies, petunias, and marigolds, the old standbys that fill in blank spaces throughout the summer months.

Contrasting foliage textures and colors work especially well when pairing roses and companion plants. Remember, creating pleasing color combinations is a matter of personal taste. There are no strict rules. If, after a while, you decide something doesn't work as expected, you can always move the offending plant and try it somewhere else. After all, rules are made to be broken. But if you need a place to start to successfully combine other plants with roses, consult the lists of suggestions on these pages. With a little bit of luck and imagination, you'll create lovely mixes of texture and color.

GOOD COMPANION PLANTS FOR ROSES

Baby's breath *(Gypsophila paniculata)*
Bellflower *(Campanula* spp.)
Boxwood *(Buxus* spp.)
Catmint *(Nepeta* spp.)
Clematis, Large-flowered hybrids
    (Clematis spp.)
Coral bells *(Heuchera* spp.)
Cottage pink *(Dianthus plumarius)*
Creeping thyme *(Thymus serpyllum)*
Dalmatian bellflower *(Campanula
    portenschlagiana)*
Foxglove *(Digitalis purpurea)*

Gaura *(Gaura lindheimeri)*
Germander *(Teucrium chamaedrys)*
Hardy geranium *(Geranium sanguineum)*
Hollyhock mallow *(Malva alcea)*
Hyssop *(Agastache* spp.)
Lady's mantle *(Alchemilla vulgaris)*
Lamb's-ears *(Stachys byzantina)*
Larkspur *(Consolida ambigua)*
Lavender *(Lavandula* spp.)
Leadwort *(Ceratostigma plumbaginoides)*
Licorice plant *(Helichrysum petiolare)*
Lily *(Lilium* spp.)

Love-in-a-Mist *(Nigella damascena)*
Milky bellflower *(Campanula lactiflora)*
Santolina *(Santolina chamaecyparissus)*
Snow-in-summer *(Cerastium tomentosum)*
Stonecrop *(Sedum spurium)*
Stonecrop *(Sedum album)*
Sweet alyssum *(Lobularia maritima)*
Thyme *(Thymus* spp.)
Twinspur *(Diascia rigescens)*
Woolly thyme *(Thymus
    pseudolanuginosus)*
Wormwood *(Artemisia* spp.)

SMALL ROSE GARDENS

A small rose garden can provide maximum impact and pleasure. Site location is vital. Select an area that gets at least six hours of sunshine a day. It can be an open area that will become an island of flowers, or it can be an area along a wall, fence, or pathway. Plan your color scheme, and then select varieties from our list of sturdy, disease-resistant, easy-to-grow roses for beginners.

Designing an island

An island bed is a circular, rectangular, or freeform design that follows contours in the landscape and is typically surrounded by lawn. The center of the bed should contain the tallest plant and be the focal point. Standard tree roses, which are about 6 feet tall, command attention. A floribunda standard tends to make a more massive display of flowers in a limited space than the one-bloom-per-stem hybrid tea. However, if you use a hybrid tea standard as the centerpiece, place a surrounding row of hybrid tea bushes about 2 to 3 feet apart. Finish off the design with a perimeter of floribundas. If the central standard tree is a floribunda, continue with a surrounding circle of floribundas, followed by a row of miniatures. Fill in with your favorite companion plants and you have created a breathtaking masterpiece.

▼ The simplest rose garden design involves a circular bed with a hybrid tea or upright floribunda in the center, surrounded by lower-growing floribundas. Ringing the bed with a closely trimmed boxwood hedge adds elegance and a finishing touch.

◀ A planting of 'Betty Prior' between a zigzagging boxwood hedge and the house foundation makes good use of limited space.

▼ Multicolored 'Joseph's Coat' provides a blaze of red, orange, and yellow as it scrambles over a white arbor and picket fence.

Creating drama at the foundation

Roses are ideal shrubs for a foundation planting. Choosing the right plants depends in large part on the depth of the bed. For instance, if the depth is 4 feet or less, a single row of floribundas all of the same variety will provide a lavish display of flowers. If the bed is 5 feet or deeper, consider training climbers on a trellis placed against the wall. Plant a row of modern shrub roses in front of the climbers, and finish off the design with medium-size floribundas in the front.

Color makes the overall design succeed. Strongly diverse colors such as red, yellow, and white make a dramatic show. Delicate pinks and whites create a softer look. Consider the color of the wall, fence, or other surface when choosing rose varieties to plant in front of it. Cerise and magenta, for example, tend to clash with the warm orangy tones of brick; a better choice is orange or salmon. Mix colors for a more relaxed, informal effect, or use a monochromatic scheme for greater formality.

LARGE GARDENS

▲ **This formal garden has triangular-shape beds defined by boxwood hedges, all pointing to a central focal point of a classic urn.**

Once you have enjoyed a small rose garden, you may be ready to move on to a larger one. A big rose garden is loaded with creative possibilities. Given adequate space, the full diversity of rose classes, shapes, sizes, colors, and forms can take center stage. Access for maintenance will be necessary, so keep that in mind. Large gardens often use mass plantings of one or two varieties to create a colorful, dramatic display (a welcome sight along walkways leading to the front door). Simple designs are often the most successful. Contour the shape of the rose beds to suit your house and its surroundings: Your choice may be square, rectangular, circular, curved, long, or short—there are no limits. Unreel your garden hose and experiment with various shapes and curves until you find one that is pleasing. If you have a large tree in the garden, consider planting Climbing 'Mlle Cécile Brünner' so it can scramble up the trunk.

Planning size and shape

Decide which types of roses are best suited to your plans based on the location of the beds and their proximity to structures. For instance, walls, fences, trellises, and arbors can be covered with climbers, ramblers, and some large shrubs. If the bed is adjacent to a wall, take a step back to gain a larger perspective. Try a terraced effect with miniatures occupying the front of the border areas. Planting different varieties at various heights creates interest in any bed, even if not in front of a wall or other structure.

Remember that standard 3-foot tree roses can be used quite effectively, but

in cold climates where roses need winter protection, standards must be shielded before freezing temperatures set in. Weeping tree roses (grafted onto either 48- or 60-inch-tall rootstock) also allow you to create impressive displays within beds using varieties known to spread out and bloom in large clusters. Try Carefree Delight (winner of the All-America Rose Selection), as well as the pink polyantha 'The Fairy' or the award-winning white miniature Gourmet Popcorn, all available as 48-inch weeping standard trees.

Using color and form

Color sets the mood of the rose garden. Bright, vibrant colors stir up excitement; pastels create a sense of peace. Contrasting colors are stimulating; harmonizing ones have a calming effect. Decide which color effect you want to achieve. Where white is the predominant color in a rose bed, you may want to include mauve, light pink, yellow, or orange. For a predominantly red rose bed, consider light pink, deep pink, coral pink, or white. In a bed of medium pink roses, complement the tranquil color scheme with light pink, deep pink, and light mauve.

A large garden is the perfect opportunity to display a wide variety of flower forms. The free-blooming, cluster-flowered floribundas offer bountiful displays of blooms. Modern shrub roses are available in so many shapes and sizes that they mix beautifully with suitable companion plants to create the look of an English cottage garden. Whatever you decide, take advantage of underused outdoor spaces and fill them with roses!

▲ **While formal in its symmetry, this garden's undulating scallops of rose beds carry a hint of informality. If you decide to pursue a large rose garden such as this one and the one on the facing page, be prepared to expend a lot of tender loving care.**

BUYING AND PLANTING ROSES

North American gardeners purchase some 60 million rose bushes each year from garden centers and mail order nurseries across the country. The vast majority of these are sold in one of two forms: bare root or in containers.

Bare-root roses are dormant plants for which soil has been removed from the roots to reduce the weight for shipping; they are sold by mail order and at some garden centers. Container roses are dormant or growing plants sold in small pots; garden centers and home improvement centers offer them from early spring until the end of the planting season, or until the available stock sells out. If you buy your roses from a mail order nursery, you will almost certainly receive bare-root roses. Miniature roses are the one exception; being lightweight, they are usually shipped in pots.

Many rose growers prefer to buy their roses by mail because the selection is greater, and they can choose the varieties they want rather than settling for ones locally available. Rarer varieties of modern roses, as well as most varieties of old garden and shrub roses, tend to be available only by mail. The biggest drawback to buying by mail is that you cannot inspect your purchases in advance. To avoid disappointment, deal only with reputable sources. Ask fellow rose gardeners for their recommendations, or use the resources listed on page 122. Reputable firms usually guarantee the safe arrival and successful growth of everything they ship, and will replace any plants that are not satisfactory. Beware of advertisements touting "low-price specials"; if something sounds too good to be true, it probably is.

Even if you are buying locally, you may prefer to purchase bare-root plants rather than potted ones. The roots of bare-root plants are typically larger than those of potted plants, because they have not been cut to fit into a container. Stripped of soil, they are also easier to inspect for general vigor and signs of damage or disease. (To keep their roots moist, some bare-root roses are wrapped in damp sphagnum peat moss and placed inside a plastic bag or a paper box. Although this prevents you from seeing the root system, you can usually feel it through a bag.) Where available, bare-root plants are sold in late winter or early spring, because they must be planted before they start to grow. For information on planting bare-root roses, see page 34.

To ensure uniform quality in rose stock, the American Association of Nurserymen, a nonprofit trade association, has established a set of standards for bare-root and potted roses. If you buy only roses that conform to these standards, you'll be assured of receiving healthy plants that will grow and bloom satisfactorily.

To conform to the standards, bare-root roses should have three or more strong canes. (An exception is polyanthas, which should have at least four canes.) The standards also specify that nurseries must allow at least two of the canes to reach a length of 18 inches, and the remaining cane or canes 13 inches, before pruning them in preparation for sale. There is no way you can know for sure that the canes actually reached these lengths, but if they extend at least 6 to 8 inches above the bud union and are about ½ inch thick, then

▲ ▼ **The rose above and the rose below are both Grade 1 because they have at least three canes ⅝ inches in diameter.**

▲ **This is a Grade 1½ bare-root rose because it has only two canes of the minimum diameter of ⅝ inch.**

you can assume that the plant is probably in good shape.

If these standards have been met, bare-root plants are known as grade number 1. This is sometimes marked on the plant's container or label and is often listed in mail order catalogs. Slightly smaller plants are known as grade number 1½. They are not as large or robust as grade number 1 plants but can usually be grown quite successfully with a little extra care. Still smaller plants are sold as grade number 2; they are rarely satisfying to rose growers.

For potted roses, the standards permit the canes of grade number 1 to be cut to 4 inches above the bud union before the plant is placed in its container; this shorter length is allowed for easier shipping. The container should be at least 2 gallons, measuring a minimum of 7 inches across the top and 7½ inches high. When buying potted roses that have already leafed out, look for three or more canes with strong, healthy leaves and additional growth buds in the area of the bud union.

With all roses, bare root or potted, the standards state that the canes should branch no more than 3 inches above the bud union. Plants should have a well-developed root system, and although the standards do not specify root size, you should choose a plant with roots that are in at least equal proportion to the aboveground part of the plant.

The standards do not address the issue of insects and diseases, but obviously you should avoid plants that show signs of insect or disease damage.

▼ **Shown below are the three most common ways roses are sold in North America: bare root, container-grown, and packaged bare root.**

◄ **Container-grown roses are increasingly popular in garden centers throughout the country. Unlike bare-root roses, they can be sold and planted all season long, even when in bloom.**

LOCATION, LOCATION, LOCATION: SUN AND AIR

▶ Roses in containers are easy to move around to where the environment is best for growing: a spot with plenty of sun and air but protection from drying wind.

▼ Sally Holmes thrives against this south-facing brick wall. In addition to the full sun, the location is extra-warm due to the heat retained by the wall.

The success of your roses depends a great deal on the conditions in which they are grown. Most roses need plenty of direct sun each day. They also need rich, fertile, and moist but well-drained soil along with good air circulation, ample growing room, and protection from harsh elements. In addition, your caretaking tasks will be easier if you can locate the plants within easy reach of your water source and the place where you store tools and supplies.

Sunlight

Roses need at least six hours of direct sun a day to grow and flower their best. Morning sun is best, since it dries off the foliage early, reducing the chance of disease. It is also less likely than afternoon sun to burn leaves and flowers, especially in hot climates.

Roses that are not receiving enough sun will show spindly growth and have thin, weak canes. Leaves will be farther apart than normal, and flower production will be poor. If these symptoms appear in your garden, you may be able to correct them by moving the plants, trimming nearby tree limbs that block the light, painting an adjacent wall or fence white to reflect available light, or by using a light-colored mulch.

Some types of roses tolerate more shade than others. Hybrid musks and miniature roses, for example, can grow and bloom in less sun than other types, about four hours of direct sun a day or the daylong dappled shadow of an ornamental tree.

Water

Although roses will survive with less than optimal watering, they will not fulfill their potential for lush growth and large, richly

colored flowers with thick, firm petals. To be sure they receive adequate moisture, locate your rose plants within reach of a hose or irrigation system, especially if you live where rainfall is unreliable.

If you are planting roses on a hillside, terrace the slope with railroad ties, landscape timbers, bricks, or stones to retard runoff and ensure that each plant receives enough water. Roses usually do not grow well in low areas where water collects and keeps the soil soggy.

Humidity

When the air around roses is extremely humid, the incidence of disease rises, since the fungal spores that attack roses thrive in high moisture. For this reason you should select a site where air can move freely. But avoid a windy location, because rapid airflow can dry out roses and tear the flowers and foliage. In humid climates, choose a spot where roses will not be closely surrounded by hedges, large plants, or walls that can constrict air movement.

Spacing

Because roses are demanding of sun, water, and nutrients, they should be placed where they will not be crowded by other plants. Keep roses at least 3 feet from the bases of other large shrubs. If possible, avoid positioning them under a tree canopy or where their roots will compete with those of other vegetation.

Roses can be interplanted with small shrubs, perennials, annuals, bulbs, and some groundcovers, such as ajuga and vinca. Be aware that roses stationed among other plants need a little more fertilizer and water.

Plant hybrid teas, floribundas, and grandifloras 24 to 30 inches apart. Plant polyanthas about 18 to 30 inches apart.

A good rule for shrub and old garden roses is to plant them as far apart as they will ultimately grow in height. In most cases, this is about 4 to 6 feet apart.

Climbers to be trained horizontally on a fence in any climate should be planted 8 to 10 feet apart. Climbers to be trained vertically up and over an arbor, or on a trellis or a wall, can be planted as close as 3 feet to create a more solid cover.

Tiny miniatures that grow only 6 inches tall should be planted about 6 inches apart. Taller ones growing to 24 inches are best spaced 12 to 18 inches apart.

▲ Roses need regular irrigation. Especially when that comes from hand watering, growing roses close to a water supply saves you extra steps.

Wind and cold protection

Although some roses can tolerate brisk conditions, most are warm-weather plants that thrive best when sheltered from wind and cold. Just as water can accumulate in low spots where drainage is poor, cold air too can collect in low areas. Try to locate roses in a part of the garden with a higher elevation. (But avoid hilltops, which are often exposed to chilling and drying winds.) If this is not possible, choose hardier roses, provide extra winter protection, or plant in a raised bed.

Easy access

An important consideration when planting roses is choosing a spot that you can easily get to and work in. If you are planting your roses against a wall or a fence, be sure you can reach the plants in the back row easily to spray, prune, or cut flowers, because walking on the bed will compact the soil. If you're planting on a hillside, plan so that you can get yourself and your equipment up and down easily.

◀ As their vigor and health indicate, these Amber Queen roses are sited in near-perfect conditions: in full sun, protected from wind by a low stone wall, and spaced about 3 feet apart for good air circulation.

GOOD SOIL FOR ROSES

Although roses can grow in any reasonably good soil, they will thrive in improved soil. The best soil for roses is fertile, moisture retentive, rich in organic matter, and loose enough to allow air and water to penetrate.

Texture

Soil is composed of sand, silt, and clay; the size of the particles determines soil texture. Sand particles are the largest, clay the smallest, and silt in between.

A soil that is too sandy cannot hold onto the water and the fertilizer you give it, so plants growing in sandy soil must be fed and watered frequently. On the positive side, the coarse texture of sandy soil provides the aeration needed for good root growth, and its fast drainage helps keep it relatively free of soilborne diseases.

Clay is a heavier soil that holds water and nutrients well, but it drains poorly because the tiny spaces between its particles do not let water through easily. Because of its compact nature, aeration is poor.

Silt, ranking between sand and clay in fineness, has both the good drainage of sand and the nutrient-holding capacity of clay. Silt is also friable (easy to work). It is almost as good as loam for growing roses, but like loam it rarely occurs naturally; it is usually found mixed with sand and clay.

The best soil of all, called loam, is a mixture of 30 to 50 percent sand, 30 to 40 percent silt, and 8 to 28 percent clay (the total must equal 100 percent). Like silt, loam drains well yet retains enough water to promote growth. It has good aeration, allowing roots to absorb oxygen and giving them room to grow, and it has excellent nutrient-retaining properties. Loose and friable, good loam is composed of 50 percent solid matter, 25 percent air, and 25 percent water.

▲ **For a quick check on your soil's texture, grab a handful of moist soil and squeeze it into a ball. Sandy soil (top) falls apart and won't hold its shape at all. Clay soil (center) remains a sticky mass when you poke it with a finger and won't break apart. Loam (bottom) and silty soil hold their shape when squeezed but readily crumble when poked.**

Acidity and alkalinity

The pH of a soil is the measure of its acidity or alkalinity—a characteristic that is independent of soil texture but that is just as essential to good plant growth. The pH of soil is expressed on a scale of 0 to 14, with the lower numbers indicating acid soil and the higher numbers alkaline (basic) soil. A pH of 7 is neutral.

In a soil that is too acidic or too alkaline, plant nutrients become insoluble and cannot be absorbed by the roots of the plant. At the same time, toxic elements are more soluble, potentially killing the plants or severely damaging their roots. Moreover, beneficial soil bacteria will not grow in highly acid or alkaline soil.

Roses grow best at a pH of 6 to 6.5. In this slightly acid range, most of the nutrients roses need are readily available. Roses will tolerate a pH as low as 5.5 or as high as 7.8, but they will not grow as well.

Testing the soil

Because there is no way to be sure what kind of soil you have by looking at it, it's a good idea to have your soil tested. This can be done by a private soil testing laboratory (check the Yellow Pages or advertisements in gardening magazines), or with soil test kits available at garden centers and agricultural supply stores. Some county extension services will also perform soil tests, or recommend laboratories.

Soil test kits usually measure only pH and thus may not reveal other, potentially serious defects of your soil. The tests done by laboratories are more complete, indicating not only pH, but also the soil texture, the amount of organic matter, the major and minor nutrients present, the level of plant toxins present, and often the corrective measures you need to take.

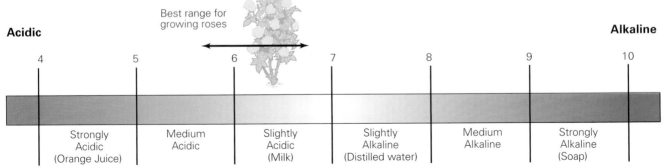

▲ **Roses grow best in soils with a pH of 6 to 6.5 (slightly acidic), the level at which they can absorb nutrients efficiently. At extreme pH values, plants suffer from improper nutrition and will be stunted. A high acidity level (below pH 6.0) produces yellow foliage on the entire plant. High alkalinity (above pH 6.5) results in yellow leaves at the top of plants.**

Improving the soil

Once an inspection and a soil test have advised you of the deficiencies of your soil, the next task is to improve it. Whether you are improving a large bed or just the soil in individual holes, the procedure is the same. First dig the soil in the area to be planted, to a depth of 16 inches. Where soil cannot be dug that deep, dig as deep as possible but at least to 8 inches. Use a hoe to break up clods of earth. To this, add 25 percent by volume of organic matter such as packaged garden soil, peat moss, leaf mold, or compost.

Avoid adding a complete granular fertilizer at this time unless you plan to leave the site unplanted for at least a month to give the fertilizer time to diffuse evenly through the soil so plant roots will not be burned.

Do, however, add a source of phosphorus, such as bonemeal, rock phosphate, or superphosphate, at the rate of 3 to 4 pounds per 100 square feet, or about 1/2 cup per planting hole. Phosphorus, which is essential for good root growth, moves very slowly through the soil. If it is applied to the top of the soil, it may take years to filter down to the root level where it is needed. The best way to get phosphorus to the root level is to put it there at the beginning.

Adjusting pH

If a soil test indicates that the pH of your soil is too low, you can raise it by adding lime (calcium carbonate). Ground dolomitic limestone (calcium magnesium carbonate) is the best type. Hydrated lime (calcium hydroxide) can burn plant roots.

If your soil is too alkaline, you can lower its pH by adding agricultural sulfur, sold

▶ Because good loam rarely occurs naturally, your soil will probably need improvement with one or more soil amendments. These are organic or inorganic materials you can mix with the soil to improve its drainage, aeration, and nutrient and water retention. Many amendments also enhance soil structure, supply nutrients, and neutralize acidity or alkalinity. Good organic amendments include packaged garden soil, sphagnum peat moss, compost, and leaf mold.

▼ Gypsum, or calcium sulfate (shown below with other amendments), is an inorganic compound used in soils with high sodium content to improve the structure of clay that does not drain well. It also forces toxic sodium to leach out.

in powder form in bags, boxes, or cans at garden centers.

Follow the package directions to determine how much lime or agricultural sulfur to apply.

Adding amendments

If there are rocks, stones, root fragments, or other debris in the soil, remove them. Spread the organic material, phosphorus source, fertilizer (if any), and any pH-adjusting material, and mix them well to the full depth you have dug; in large areas, a rotiller is helpful in breaking up large clods of soil and incorporating the amendments. The total soil volume will be greater after you have mixed in the amendments.

It is best, although not always practical, to improve the soil one to six months before planting, as this allows the soil to mellow and settle and the pH to become properly adjusted. It also lessens the chance that fresh organic matter or fertilizers will burn the roots of new plants.

Soil should be improved only if it is in workable condition; that is, fairly dry and friable. To test the workability of your soil, pick up a handful and squeeze it into a ball. If the soil sticks together, it is too wet. Wait several days and perform the test again. Soil is ready to be worked when it crumbles in your hand when you squeeze it.

GUIDE TO PLANTING FOR SUCCESS

PLANTING BARE-ROOT ROSES

1 Check the planting hole to make sure it's the right depth. Remove most of the soil from the hole. Make a pyramid at the bottom of the hole with the remaining soil.

2 Test the height of the pyramid by setting the bare-root bush on it, then laying a broomstick across the top to make sure the bud union is at the correct level. Gently spread the bare roots over the cone of soil.

3 Carefully add the remaining soil to cover the roots, leaving a 4-inch gap at the top of the hole.

4 Water the plant slowly so the soil can begin to settle. Water carefully several more times to let the soil fill in completely. Add soil to the hole to bring it to the proper level and water again.

5 Mound mulch over the exposed bud union or base of the plant to prevent moisture loss. Make a soil dam around the plant to collect water.

6 After a few weeks of careful watering and when the roots are established, buds and leaves will appear. It is now time to begin removing the protective mound of mulch over the bud union or base of the plant.

7 Each time you water the rose, gently wash away some of the mulch mound until the bud union is at the proper level.

Most often, roses, whether old or modern, arrive in your garden as dormant, bare-root plants, but they can also be purchased as potted, container-grown specimens.

Planting bare-root roses

You can purchase bare-root roses at a local nursery or order them by mail. A bare-root rose looks stark, with stubby, thorny stems and stiff roots growing from a rough knob. The knob is the bud union, where the roots and main stem were grafted together. (Many old garden roses are grown on their own roots and do not have a graft union.)

These bare roots need a good soaking in water before you set them in the ground—they need to store up moisture that can be lost during planting. Soak them for two to three hours prior to planting in a bucket of water. Next, trim off any broken roots, but avoid cutting back the canes unless they are damaged. Fresh cuts allow moisture to escape. If any canes are damaged, however, trim them below the damage. Finally, immediately prior to planting dip the bare roots for a minute or so in a solution of one tablespoon of bleach per gallon of water. This will help remove any pests or spores that might remain on the plant.

With the advance work done—including the soil preparation steps described on pages 32–33—you're ready to plant your roses. First, remove most of the soil from the prepared planting hole. Make a cone of soil in the center to accommodate the roots and spread them out evenly over the cone (if one or two roots are too long, trim them to fit the hole). Check the height of the bud union with a broomstick laid across the hole, and adjust the cone of soil to keep the bud union at the correct level for your climate. As a general rule, plant the bud union 2 to 3 inches belowground in cold-winter climates (lows below –10° F), and at ground level or slightly above where winter lows are –10° F or warmer.

Add the remaining soil, firming it as you go, and water it to help it settle in. Mound the plant with 8 to 12 inches of mulch, and encircle it with a dam of soil to help collect water. Water it well every three to four days to get the roots off to a healthy start. When the root structure is established (in about three weeks), remove the mound of mulch a little at a time. In four to five weeks the bud eyes should be swollen and about to burst. Watch for wrinkling on the canes—the first sign of dehydration. If this occurs, recut the canes below the wrinkling, remound the plant, and water well.

Planting container-grown roses

Container-grown roses have become increasingly popular; they can be planted during bare-root season and also later in the season. Pot-grown roses are also somewhat easier to plant—you don't need to make the cone of soil for the roots, for example.

Before you plant the rose, gradually reduce its water (a process called hardening off) for a week. But on planting day, make sure the container soil (and the soil in the hole you've dug) is moist. Reducing its water beforehand will help prepare the rose for the transplant, and watering at planting time will help keep the root ball together and reduce stress caused by the surrounding dry ground absorbing moisture away from the roots.

Follow the simple steps illustrated at right for removing the container and planting the rose bush. Remember to keep the bud union at the height it would be if it were a bare-root plant. Refill the planting hole with soil dug from it. Press the soil gently around the root ball, but do not stamp it with your feet. Water the soil in to settle it, adding more soil if necessary. Then water once more with a solution of liquid starter fertilizer and vitamin B-1. Be sure to keep the soil moist during the first season, until the roots are well established.

PLANTING CONTAINER-GROWN ROSES

PREPARE THE HOLE

If your soil is in good shape, dig the hole as deep as the container. If you are planting in poor soil, dig the hole twice as wide and deep as the container, and amend the soil as needed.

LOOSEN THE ROOTBALL IN THE CONTAINER

Place the container on its side on a hard surface and roll from side to side while gently pushing or squeezing the container.

REMOVE THE CONTAINER

While holding the soil at the base of the rose with one hand, tip the pot and gently slide out the root ball, keeping the soil intact around the roots. Carefully place the root ball in the hole.

BACKFILL, CREATE A BASIN, AND WATER IN.

Create a basin around the planting hole by mounding soil into a dam. Water, allow the soil to settle, and if necessary add more soil. Then water again.

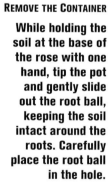

Planting Roses in Containers

Growing roses in containers is a practical way to make the most of your garden space. You can display them when they are blooming and remove them when they are bare and severely pruned. Roses in containers can also add decorative touches around the garden or on the patio, porch, or deck.

Because roses grown in containers are showcase plants, choose varieties that are compact and free flowering for maximum visual appeal. You can plant either bare-root or container-grown roses, but the latter seem to get a better start because their roots are already growing in a confined space.

Choosing a container

For all roses, too little root space leads to stunted growth and poor flower production. For full-size rose bushes, the ideal container is in the 15- to 20-gallon range (about the size of a half whiskey barrel) to provide roots with adequate growing space. A container 18 inches across and deep is a minimum size. Containers for miniature roses should be in the 5- to 7-gallon range (a minimum of 12 inches across and deep). Because their roots tend to spread out, miniature roses grow best in containers that are wider than they are tall.

Containers can be made of a variety of materials, including wood, clay, concrete, or plastic. Stay away from metal containers for outdoor growing, because they absorb too much heat and can stifle growth. Whatever type of container you use, be sure it drains adequately; rose roots do not like to sit in water. Choose a container with drainage holes at the bottom or on the sides near the bottom. If a saucer is used, the pot must not be allowed to stand in a water-filled saucer or roots may rot. Avoid pots with tightly-fitting saucers that do not allow for adequate drainage or removal of water.

If drainage holes are absent and cannot be drilled, plant the rose in a smaller container that has holes and set it inside the larger container. Place a layer of gravel at the bottom of the solid container to raise the inner container above the drainage water. You can grow a large rose in a container that lacks drainage holes by placing a deep layer of gravel and charcoal in the bottom, but you must take great care not to overwater.

If you are reusing a container, clean the vessel thoroughly so that any disease organisms will not be transmitted to the new plants. Scrub the pot with warm, soapy water, and rinse it well with clear water. Then rinse the container in a 10 percent solution of household bleach to disinfect it, and rinse it with water again.

Roses in Hanging Baskets

One effective way to make a hanging basket is to use a container that is much wider than it is deep. This permits the plant to generate a strong root system, because the roots are protected from heat. The wide container also helps to support the canes before they start drooping over the edge.

Because a hanging basket is suspended and exposed, it needs a 1- to 2-inch lining of peat moss as a protective barrier against moisture loss on hot days. Hanging baskets need to be watered more frequently than plants in the ground, and the soil mix should never be allowed to dry out. Plastic self-watering hanging pots that incorporate a sizable water-holding chamber are an excellent choice to minimize watering. However, because they lack drainage, locate them where they won't be rained on.

Planting a rose in a container

Because root space is so limited in a container and roots cannot forage far and wide for water, nutrients, and oxygen, plants growing in containers especially need the right kind of growing medium. It is best to avoid native soil from your garden. No matter how well amended and earthworm laden your soil is, it is too heavy for roses in containers and will not provide optimal drainage and aeration. Native soil can also harbor harmful insects and diseases. Instead, use one of the all-purpose, premium soil mixes available in bags and packages at garden centers.

Set the plant in the container in the same way that you would plant it in the ground, positioning the bud union or crown at the soil level, about 1 inch below the rim of the container. Water well.

Container culture

Place the container where it will receive at least six hours of sun each day. Avoid putting it where it will become too hot, such as on asphalt pavement or against a highly reflective wall. Feed regularly with a plant food formulated for roses, and keep the roots evenly moist. In hot weather you may need to water daily.

When a rose outgrows its container, it needs to be repotted. Check the soil's surface to see whether it is dense with roots. If the plant wilts even when you water frequently, then it is probably time to repot. To repot, remove the plant from its pot, clean some of the soil off the roots, and prune the roots by one-third. Then replant in a container that is a few inches larger than the old one. Be sure to use fresh potting mix. Roses grow quickly and may need repotting every two or three years.

In Zones 3 through 7 avoid leaving plants or containers outside over winter. Plant roses, container and all, in the ground and mulch well, or bring them into a cool, frost-free location such as an attached garage.

◄ Plastic pots are light and inexpensive and often require less watering than porous terra-cotta and wood, which let water pass through their walls. The evaporation helps keep roots cool, but plants need watering more frequently. Miniature roses need pots in the 5- to 7-gallon range; larger roses need more room—at least 15 to 20 gallons, about half the size of a whiskey barrel.

▲ If the container you are using to grow a rose doesn't have drainage holes, you will need to add them. It is easy to drill holes in most wood and plastic pots. For ceramic pots, use a masonry bit.

A Guide to Healthy Roses

▼ Gardeners demand a lot from roses—vigorous growth that resists pests and diseases, and remarkable summer-long blooms. This high performance takes plenty of food and water. Plan on a regular program of feeding and irrigation. See pages 40–42.

The care you give your roses on a daily basis has long-term effects on their health and flowering. Although roses make more demands than the average garden plant, they are not especially difficult to grow. All that is required is a basic command of a few simple techniques.

This chapter describes in detail feeding, watering, grooming, mulching, weeding, and putting your roses to bed for the winter. Complete instructions for pruning all kinds of roses are presented, as well as The Ortho Rose Problem Solver— a special guide to preventing, identifying, and treating problems caused by insects and diseases. The chapter concludes with a complete month-by-month calendar of rose care for every USDA Hardiness Zone in North America.

Some roses are easier to care for than others. For example, some old garden roses and many shrubs demand less care than do hybrid teas and grandifloras, because they need less pruning and are not as susceptible to diseases. Recent breeding has resulted in new landscape roses that are highly resistant to diseases, are self-cleaning, do not produce hips (so they need no deadheading), and bloom repeatedly all season. For example, Knock Out, introduced by Bill Radler in 1999, has revolutionized rose growing because it is virtually immune to black spot. Since that time Mr. Radler has introduced a series of progeny also highly resistant to the fungal disease, including Pink Knockout, Double Knockout, Double Pink Knockout, and the yellow Carefree Sunshine.

If you're concerned about finding time to tend a rose garden, start small; any garden can support even a few bushes. As you become experienced, you can add to your garden and increase your enjoyment of the "Queen of Flowers."

▽ **Pruning is no mystery—by mastering a few simple techniques you can enjoy maximum flower production and vigorous, well-shaped plants. See pages 44–49.**

▷ **Protecting rose plants from pests and diseases is a matter of regular preventive care. Detecting and identifying a pest early before it becomes a serious problem is the key. See pages 52–59.**

FEEDING ROSES

▶ You water and feed your roses at the same time when you apply liquid fertilizer with a hose-end applicator. The fertilizer is taken up by both foliage and roots for quick effect without burning plants.

Well-fed roses reach their full size, produce abundant flowers, and stay healthy, resisting attack from insects and diseases. What you feed your roses, and how often, depends to some extent on your soil. Roses grown in sandy soil may need more frequent feeding than those grown in loam or heavier soil.

Roses need three primary nutrients—nitrogen (the N on a fertilizer label), phosphorus (P) and potassium (K)—as well as a number of secondary and trace elements in order to thrive. Nitrogen promotes leafy growth, phosphorus encourages healthy root and flower development, and potassium maintains vigor. Calcium, magnesium, and sulfur (secondary elements) and boron, copper, and iron (trace elements) also promote plant cell and root growth.

Primary nutrients are available from both organic (derived from plant or animal life) and synthetic, or inorganic, materials. Synthetic fertilizers come in dry, liquid, or foliar liquid form. Dry fertilizer is worked into the soil (moistened first) and is watered in well to carry the nutrients to the roots. Liquid fertilizer is added to water with a hose-end applicator, and foliar liquid is sprayed on and absorbed by the leaves. Whatever you use, be sure to follow the directions and dosages exactly. Excessive doses can damage plants.

Most roses need regular feeding—with fertilizers that are balanced for roses, your region, and your garden soil. Begin fertilizing newly planted roses once they

HOW TO READ A LABEL

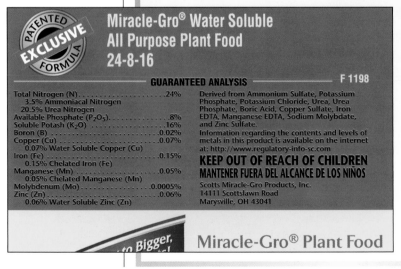

Miracle-Gro® Water Soluble All Purpose Plant Food
24-8-16

PATENTED EXCLUSIVE FORMULA

GUARANTEED ANALYSIS   F 1198

Total Nitrogen (N) 24%
   3.5% Ammoniacal Nitrogen
   20.5% Urea Nitrogen
Available Phosphate (P_2O_5) 8%
Soluble Potash (K_2O) 16%
Boron (B) 0.02%
Copper (Cu) 0.07%
   0.07% Water Soluble Copper (Cu)
Iron (Fe) 0.15%
   0.15% Chelated Iron (Fe)
Manganese (Mn) 0.05%
   0.05% Chelated Manganese (Mn)
Molybdenum (Mo) 0.0005%
Zinc (Zn) 0.06%
   0.06% Water Soluble Zinc (Zn)

Derived from Ammonium Sulfate, Potassium Phosphate, Potassium Chloride, Urea, Urea Phosphate, Boric Acid, Copper Sulfate, Iron EDTA, Manganese EDTA, Sodium Molybdate, and Zinc Sulfate.
Information regarding the contents and levels of metals in this product is available on the internet at: http://www.regulatory-info-sc.com
KEEP OUT OF REACH OF CHILDREN
MANTENER FUERA DEL ALCANCE DE LOS NIÑOS
Scotts Miracle-Gro Products, Inc.
14111 Scottslawn Road
Marysville, OH 43041

Miracle-Gro® Plant Food

A Guaranteed Analysis statement must appear on all mixed fertilizer labels. The label must indicate the proportion of each element present, as well as its sources (in this example, urea, ammonium phosphate, potassium phosphate, and so on). The numbers 24-8-16 denote the percentages of the components containing nitrogen, phosphorus, and potassium in this mix. This package contains 24 percent ammoniacal nitrogen and urea nitrogen, 8 percent phosphate, and 16 percent soluble potash. Some fertilizers also contain secondary nutrients and micronutrients. Look for fertilizers with micronutrients derived from EDTA complexes. as they are water soluble and thus immediately available to the root system. In some cases, a soil penetrant is added to the fertilizer to assist in delivering nutrients into clay soils.

▲ Slow-release fertilizer provides good plant nutrition over a long period, for up to four months. It works best during warm weather, when daytime temperatures are consistently over 70°F.

◄ Granular fertilizer balanced for roses should be applied directly to the soil around each bush, cultivated lightly, and watered in.

are established—about three to four weeks after planting. Start feeding older plants in spring when new growth is about 3 inches long. At a minimum, species roses, old garden roses, and climbers need a feeding in early spring as the buds prepare to open. Repeat-blooming roses, old garden roses, and climbers benefit from a second feeding of liquid fertilizer after the first bloom, and modern roses need regular feeding.

Watering and fertilizing at the same time

Hose-end sprayers designed to apply liquid fertilizer are handy gadgets that allow you to dispense a measured amount of water-soluble fertilizer as you water. To use a hose-end sprayer, add fertilizer to the reservoir as directed on the label and spray the foliage and the soil beneath the plants. The sprayer contains a built-in proportioner that applies the correct amount of fertilizer at the correct dilution. Some models allow you to attach wands, sprinklers, or other watering devices for added convenience. When feeding roses, be sure to use only hose-end sprayers made specifically for applying fertilizers.

Given proper feeding, roses will generally provide bloom cycles, or intervals between peak bloom production, about every 50 days. When the first bloom cycle is

complete, initiating the second crop of roses, the nutrient needs of the rose garden change dramatically. Feed once a week or at least every two weeks to maintain the health and productivity of the bush. Use a high-nitrogen, water-soluble fertilizer with an N-P-K of 8-10-8 to 20-20-20 (1 tablespoon per gallon, delivering about 2 gallons per mature bush and about 1 gallon per younger plant). Or broadcast about ¼ cup of granular fertilizer around hybrid tea bushes and water it in.

Alfalfa pellets worked into the soil are a good organic source of nitrogen and can be used as a slow-release supplement in spring. Avoid pellets that are feed grade so your rose food doesn't feed the rabbits. A time-release synthetic fertilizer applied in spring and again in July will reduce the need for reapplications.

In Zone 7 and colder areas, stop fertilizing six weeks before the average date of the first frost and let plants harden off for their winter rest.

FERTILIZING ROSES IN CONTAINERS

The increased watering required for container roses also leaches nutrients from the soil more quickly, and you will have to fertilize more often to make up for the loss. With both liquid and dry fertilizers, apply half as much twice as often (half strength of a water-soluble fertilizer, for example, every two weeks) but avoid over-fertilizing. If you mistakenly overdo it, soak the plant thoroughly to wash out the excess.

WATERING ROSES

Water is vital in delivering nutrients to roses. It travels up canes depositing nutrients for leaf, stem, and flower growth, and it goes down canes to build strong roots.

Roses lose water from leaf pores in a process known as transpiration. When underwatered roots can't keep up with the watering needs of the plant, leaves and young stems wilt. Overwatering, on the other hand, starves roots of oxygen, and the lower leaves turn yellow and fall off. Normally, you should give your roses 1 to 2 inches of water each week—in a single watering session—from early spring through fall. Increase the frequency to every three or four days in hot and dry weather. Porous soils also benefit from additional deep soakings.

WATERING ROSES IN CONTAINERS

Roses grown in containers need more attention than those grown in the ground because they have less soil from which to draw moisture.

Check the moisture depth in the pot at least every one or two days during the summer—every day when the weather is hot or windy. Unglazed pots lose moisture more quickly than those made of plastic or glazed pottery. You can put one container inside another to reduce moisture loss, but be sure the outside container has drainage holes too.

A microirrigation system with ring emitters is a convenient method for watering containers.

▲ A bubbler attachment allows water to soak slowly into the soil.

▲ A soaker hose, which waters slowly and gently, can water several bushes at the same time.

▲ Plants that are overwatered are starved of oxygen; their lower foliage turns yellow and falls off.

▲ The succulent young stems and leaves of underwatered plants tend to droop and sag.

Soak the soil to a 16- to 18-inch depth; light sprinkling does more harm than not watering at all, because the roots will fail to grow deep enough to support the plant. Lightly watered plants are more easily injured by cultivation and are also more susceptible to fertilizer burn. Check the depth of your watering. Water for a measured length of time and dig near the roots. If the soil is moist to a depth of only 8 inches, you should water twice as long.

Methods of applying water

There are several options for applying water, among them drip irrigation, underground sprinklers, and hand watering.

Drip, or low-volume, irrigation is an efficient method that releases water to your plant without runoff. You can place an emitter on each side of a plant, use manufactured drip collars, or fashion your own collar with perforated drip tubing.

Conventional spray heads direct water up onto the foliage, removing spider mites, which live on the underside of the leaves. Low-volume minisprays apply water more economically, but do a poorer job of wetting the foliage.

If you're hand watering, you may want to consider using a bubbler attachment. Flooding a basin around the rose allows water to soak slowly into soil and prevents a strong stream from eroding the soil or splashing dirt. Bubbler heads attached to an underground system accomplish this task even more conveniently.

Apply a 2- to 4-inch layer of mulch on top of the soil to slow the evaporation of water. Mulching also insulates the ground in winter so it freezes and thaws gradually, which prevents plants from heaving out of the soil.

GROOMING, WEEDING, MULCHING, AND CLEANING

Roses love attention and care. With regular grooming, weeding, and a little picking up after them, your roses will resist diseases and insects and reward you season after season.

After the first and second bloom cycles, remove spent blossoms. This process, called deadheading, allows the plant to channel its energy into producing more blooms instead of seed. Deadheaded plants rebloom more quickly, are likely to grow stronger stems, and generally look more attractive. Cut the spent blossom back to the nearest five leaflets where the stem is about as thick as a pencil. Make sure the swollen bud eye (on which the new flower stem will grow) points to the outside of the bush. Leave as much foliage on the bush as possible. After deadheading, the leaflet at the cut may turn yellow and fall off. This is normal.

How to disbud roses

If you're growing grandifloras and floribundas, a practice called disbudding can produce spectacular results. These roses normally bloom in clusters; the central flower blooms first, followed by the secondary buds. The central flower inhibits the development of the lower side buds. Removing it allows the surrounding buds to burst into a larger display.

The summer months are an ideal time to open up the central area of each bush to improve air circulation and suppress fungal diseases. Remove twiggy growth not capable of supporting new growth. Cut such weak growth all the way back to the main cane or stem. While this loss of

HOW TO MULCH ROSES

Besides helping to retain moisture, mulching is an effective weed control and reduces the need for cultivation, which, if done too deeply (more than 1 to 1½ inches), can damage feeder roots. You can apply mulch to single plants or over a whole bed. Organic mulches, such as bark, grass clippings, rotted manure, straw, and shredded leaves, break down and improve the soil. Landscape fabric blocks light that weeds need for germination but lets water through. After planting, apply 2 to 4 inches of mulch, but avoid mounding mulch around the base of plants. If you have problems with fungal diseases, remove the mulch each fall. In cold-winter regions, wait until the soil warms to replace mulch.

GOOD MULCH

Redwood (small bark)	Straw	Pine straw
Mushroom compost	Shredded tree leaves	Cocoa bean shells
Rotted manures	Pine needles	Rice hulls
Earthworm castings	Aged sawdust	Ground corncobs
	Compost	Grass clippings

▶ **Preemergence herbicide is an easy way to prevent weed seedlings from germinating.**

foliage surface is not always desirable, the benefits of its removal are worthwhile. Now is also an ideal opportunity to remove any deadwood or dying stems.

Remove weeds at the first sign of growth; once they become established they're stubborn. Suppress them with landscape fabric, mulch, or a preemergence herbicide, and pull any that do appear before they get a foothold. Exercise caution when using an herbicide spray. If it drifts onto rose foliage, it might cause dwarfed and wrinkled foliage or even kill the plant. Remove dead foliage and other leaf litter from the beds; such material is a haven for pests and fungal spores that could plague the rose bush later in the summer.

HOW TO DISBUD AND GROOM A HYBRID TEA

To achieve maximum flower size, remove any secondary buds that might develop around a central bud.

HOW TO DISBUD AND GROOM A GRANDIFLORA OR A FLORIBUNDA SPRAY

To achieve maximum flower effect in a spray or open cluster, disbud the central bud after it appears. The remaining florets in the spray will all bloom at the same time.

THE BASICS OF ROSE PRUNING

BEST TIMES TO PRUNE

Begin pruning after spring's last frost. Here are some representative cities and the suggested pruning times for each:

Atlanta: early March
Boston: late April
Chicago: early April
Dallas: late March
Los Angeles: early January
St. Louis: late March
Seattle: early April
Washington: early March

Pruning basics

Of all gardening chores, pruning seems to create the most anxiety. It need not be that way. You can learn the rudiments from books and demonstrations, as you can any skill, but it's your own hands-on experience that will translate that information into working knowledge. If you make a few mistakes, they won't result in disaster; your rose will still perform. And as you get to know your roses, proper pruning will enhance your enjoyment and pride in helping nature present its best. Approach pruning like an artist—after all, you're about to create a masterpiece. Try to imagine what the bush will look like. Let your inspiration flow.

Pruning gives you the opportunity each year to correct, adjust, and modify the growth of your roses to increase their flower production. Pruning times and techniques will vary somewhat with the types of roses in your garden and where you live. (See page 48 for a discussion of pruning practices for each variety.) But in all cases pruning enhances the architecture of the plant, ensures a vigorous first bloom, and encourages new growth. Removing old and damaged wood allows the plant to recuperate. In warmer climates pruning is necessary to induce a kind of dormancy that cold-weather plants receive in winter. Even roses need a rest. During this period, plant growth is slowed and redirected toward producing those first magnificent blooms.

When and how much should you prune? Here are some guidelines. In general, you will be pruning just before the plant breaks dormancy after spring's final frost. This will be early in the year in warm climates, and anytime between January and April in cold climates. If you are tending old roses, prune them after they bloom; they bear flowers on last year's wood. With any rose, cut away the deadwood first—it will help you see the shape of the plant without distraction.

It's a good idea to visit a public rose garden and find specimens of roses you are growing. Note how the gardeners have pruned roses of the same type. In cold-winter climates, pruning is often reduced to one option: Cut back the wood that was killed in winter. In warm climates, pruning can be done at any of three levels, depending on your purpose. Severe pruning (leave three or four canes, 6 to 10 inches tall) produces fewer but larger blooms. Moderate pruning (leave five to 12 canes 18 to 24 inches) makes for a larger bush. And light pruning (less than one-third of the plant is thinned) increases the number of short-stemmed flowers that will be produced.

WHY PRUNE?

By fall, miniature roses have grown tall and leggy. Colder evenings produce ill-formed, mottled blossoms and yellowing foliage that often starts to fall off (below left). Rose hips, which can interrupt the next blooming cycle, may result if spent blossoms are not removed. Pruning removes diseased and dead stems and canes and reduces the overall size of the plant (below center). The first spring bloom demonstrates how pruning results in an annual process of renewal (below right).

▲ Miniature plant as it looks in the late fall.

▲ After pruning in late winter.

▲ The first spring bloom.

The right tools

Invest in a pair of high-quality pruning shears with both blades curved. (Those with a flat "anvil" on one blade tend to crush stems, not cut them.) This is one tool where price really does make a difference. Select a manufacturer with a proven track record, and buy the best that you can afford. Some pruning shears have a special hand grip designed for left-handed people. Others have swivel handles that are easier on your wrists, and there are models with removable blades for storage. Smaller versions (costing about $20) are available for pruning miniature roses. Next, you'll need a pair of lopping shears. Loppers are pruning shears with long (12- to 18-inch) handles that will provide leverage for the thicker canes. The third tool is a pruning saw to remove large woody canes: It will give you a clean cut without damage to the bud union. Finally, buy a good strong pair of leather gauntlet gloves or gloves that are punctureproof. Now, you're ready to start pruning.

PROPER PRUNING TECHNIQUES

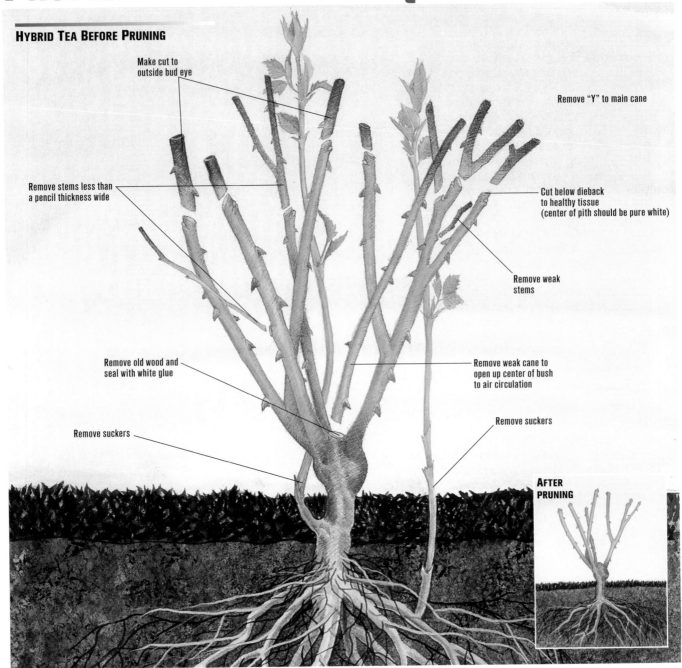

HYBRID TEA BEFORE PRUNING

Make cut to outside bud eye

Remove "Y" to main cane

Remove stems less than a pencil thickness wide

Cut below dieback to healthy tissue (center of pith should be pure white)

Remove weak stems

Remove old wood and seal with white glue

Remove weak cane to open up center of bush to air circulation

Remove suckers

Remove suckers

AFTER PRUNING

General tips for proper pruning

1. Always prune dead wood back to healthy tissue. You will recognize the living tissue by its green bark and white pith, or core.

2. If you live in an area where cane borers are a severe problem, provide protection from cane borer larvae tunneling into the center of cut stems by covering each cut with a drop of white glue.

3. Prune to ensure the center of the bush is open for maximum air circulation.

4. Remove any growth on the main canes that is not capable of sustaining a reasonably thick stem on its own.

5. If suckers—growths from the roots that sprout from below the bud union—are present, remove them as close to the main root cane as possible.

6. Remove old woody canes; saw them off as close to the bud union as you can get.

7. After you have completed pruning your rose bush, remove any remaining foliage from the canes and clean up debris from around the bush. Discard all foliage (keep it out of the compost heap).

Good Cuts, Bad Cuts

By far the most important rose-pruning technique to master is the art of the correct angle. Make your pruning cuts at a 45-degree angle, about ¼ inch above a leaf axil with a dormant bud eye. Choose an eye on the outside of the cane and slope the cut down and away on the opposite side. This allows excess natural water to rise and seal the cut without interfering with the developing eye. Pruning to an outward-facing bud also promotes outward growth, opens up the plant to air circulation and makes it more disease resistant, creates a more pleasing shape, and prevents the canes from becoming a tangle. A cut closer to the eye than ¼ inch may damage it, and a cut higher than that will leave a visible stub—a haven for both pests and diseases.

If the rose bush has foliage on it, the location is easy to spot. Where there are no leaves to guide you, find the dormant bud eye by locating where the foliage was once connected. The eye is normally visible as a slight swelling rising above the surface of the cane.

Use this same pruning technique when cutting stems for display and when removing spent blooms. Remember to sharpen your pruning tools periodically—either do it yourself or have someone who's specially trained do it. Wipe metal surfaces after each use with a soft, lightly oiled rag to prevent rust. Store tools in a dry area. Master these simple rules and your spring rose growth is guaranteed to produce a pleasing overall shape and habit for the rest of the season.

Making the Right Cut

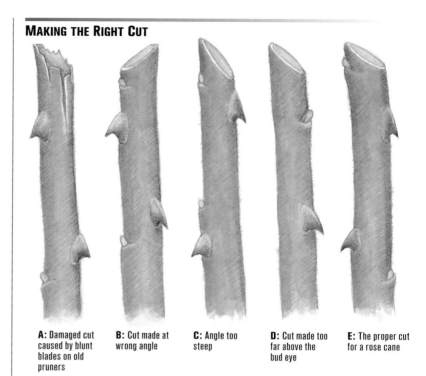

A: Damaged cut caused by blunt blades on old pruners

B: Cut made at wrong angle

C: Angle too steep

D: Cut made too far above the bud eye

E: The proper cut for a rose cane

Finding the Dormant Bud Eye

Look for a slight swelling resembling a small pimple where the foliage has fallen off the cane. That's the dormant bud eye that will produce a new stem.

Why It's Important to Make the Correct Cut

When the cut is made correctly—here, above an aging five-leaflet set with a dormant bud eye below—the water will rise from the rose cane and run

down its opposite side. Remove the old leaf set just below the cut. Within a few weeks the dormant bud eye will begin to swell. In another three weeks

the swelling will result in a young new stem showing just a few foliage sets. Eventually that growth will become a stem and bloom.

PRUNING ROSES IN MILD CLIMATES

Now that you're acquainted with the pruning basics, you're ready to apply them to your roses. The following instructions pertain to roses grown in mild-winter climates. The pruning differences for each variety don't apply to cold-winter gardeners because of the dieback caused by the cold. For cold-winter pruning instructions, see the box "Pruning in a Harsh Winter Climate" at right.

Hybrid teas and grandifloras

By winter, hybrid tea roses and grandifloras are generally 5 to 7 feet tall and looking rather lanky. You can prune the canes (on an established bush) 2 to 4 feet but, in general, leave four to five major canes with an average height of 3 feet. Removing older canes will trigger the rose bush to attempt basal breaks (new cane growth) in the spring. This regenerative process is fundamental to the health of the bush.

Floribundas and polyanthas

Since these types of roses are mainly for garden display rather than cut flowers, you can allow more older canes to remain for increased flower production. Cut back about one-third of the year's new growth and leave substantially more stems than you would for a hybrid tea (see illustration, below). By nature, floribundas and polyanthas produce large numbers of flowers. Leaving a greater number of canes enhances the ability of the rose bush to produce the maximum number of flowers.

HOW TO PRUNE A FLORIBUNDA

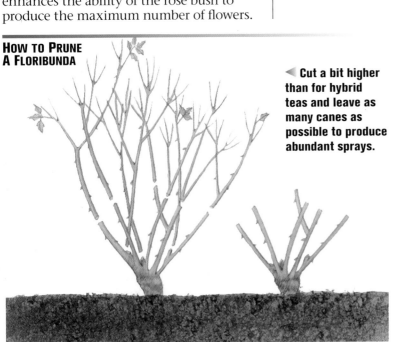

◀ Cut a bit higher than for hybrid teas and leave as many canes as possible to produce abundant sprays.

PRUNING IN A HARSH WINTER CLIMATE

In colder climates, most of the pruning advice given here still applies. Northerners just don't have as many height decisions to make. Where winter snow and freezing temperatures are commonplace, precise pruning for each variety is not necessary because—in spite of the winter protection measures—canes will die in the cold and must be cut back severely.

Remove all diseased and dead, blackened canes, and then prune a little more off each remaining cane until you see center pith that is creamy white, not brownish. Remove any weak, twiggy growth and canes that cross each other and rub in the wind. Then stand back and admire what you have left and be glad that your severe winter also killed most insects and disease-causing fungi. Two additional thoughts to keep in mind: Never prune in the fall, as it encourages new growth and even more winterkill; and, in spring, wait until all danger of severe weather is past before uncovering and pruning your roses. As the old saying goes, when the forsythia blooms, it is time to prune.

Miniature roses

Most miniatures are grown on their own roots; there is no bud union, so there are no suckers. Precise pruning of miniature roses is labor intensive, and many rosarians simply use a hedge clipper to trim the tops about 1 foot above the soil (height depends on the variety). After such treatment, remove any twiggy growth and open up the center of the plant to increase air circulation.

Old garden roses and shrubs

Old garden roses are not treated like modern hybrid teas or floribundas. For maximum blooms, give them more of a light grooming than a severe cutback. Prune only the previous year's growth. Prune one-time bloomers immediately after flowering; prune repeat bloomers in winter or early spring. After a few years, however, this practice makes for a lanky bush, so each year thereafter prune back some of the oldest canes to promote the development of new stems near the crown (or, for grafted roses, the bud union). Keeping a proper balance between new growth and

HOW TO PRUNE A CLIMBER:

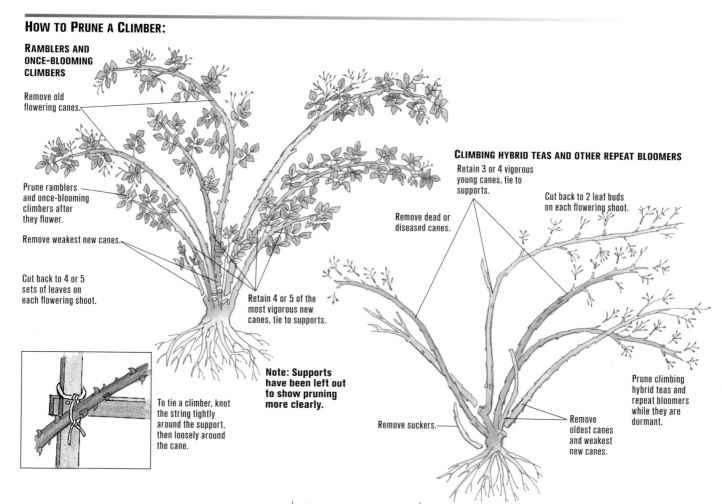

RAMBLERS AND ONCE-BLOOMING CLIMBERS

Remove old flowering canes.

Prune ramblers and once-blooming climbers after they flower.

Remove weakest new canes.

Cut back to 4 or 5 sets of leaves on each flowering shoot.

To tie a climber, knot the string tightly around the support, then loosely around the cane.

Retain 4 or 5 of the most vigorous new canes, tie to supports.

Note: Supports have been left out to show pruning more clearly.

CLIMBING HYBRID TEAS AND OTHER REPEAT BLOOMERS

Retain 3 or 4 vigorous young canes, tie to supports.

Remove dead or diseased canes.

Cut back to 2 leaf buds on each flowering shoot.

Prune climbing hybrid teas and repeat bloomers while they are dormant.

Remove suckers.

Remove oldest canes and weakest new canes.

---

continuing old growth patterns is the secret to growing old garden roses.

Climbers and ramblers

Climbers generally will not flower profusely unless the canes are trained horizontally. Cut the long-established canes to about where they are slightly thicker than a pencil. Then cut each side stem that has flowered to the lowest possible five-leaflet stem, about 1 to 2 inches from the main cane. This process will cause the cane to flower along its complete length.

After pruning

Follow these suggestions to reduce the potential for disease as well as to encourage vigorous new growth:

1. Thoroughly clean the rose beds of dead leaves and other debris. You will reduce the potential for insects and fungi to survive the winter by eliminating the places where they hide. Bag all the material you've pruned; keep rose clippings out of mulch and compost because fungal spores can invade the stems and cause reinfections when warmer weather returns.

▲ **Train the long canes into a horizontal position. Cut back flowering shoots, leaving four or five leaf sets. These small branches will produce next year's flowers. Canes older than four or five years should be removed to induce new growth.**

2. To ensure the destruction of all insect pests and fungi, apply a dormant pesticide or fungicide spray such as ORTHO Volck Oil Spray immediately after pruning—when there are no bud eyes developing. Use the old-fashioned oil-and-sulfur spray to help destroy both powdery mildew and downy mildew spores residing in the soil and on the canes. Inorganic sulfur compounds are available at garden centers; follow instructions on the label to mix the sulfur with horticultural oil.

3. After brushing the bud union with a wire brush to remove the old bark, cover it with about 6 to 10 inches of mulch. This protective mound of mulch keeps the bud union moist and receptive to new canes. Additionally, the mound can protect the bud union from mild frost and wind chill. Many rose experts avoid this step, however, believing it promotes crown gall, a plant disease.

4. Avoid feeding roses until about three or four weeks after pruning. At that time, apply a balanced granular rose food around the base of the mound covering the bud union, and then uncover the bud union. The mulch provides a clean landscaping surface to start the new year.

PROTECTING FROM THE ELEMENTS

ROSE CONE PROTECTION

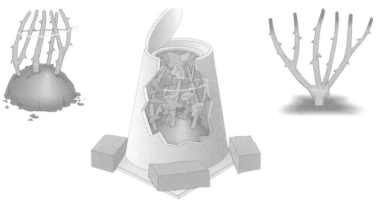

T he first maxim of winter protection: Select plants that are hardy to winter in your area so you won't have to worry about protecting them. One of the most important aspects of selection is to buy roses budded onto a rootstock that will survive your climate—for example, multiflora for Zone 6 and colder areas—and to plant the bud union at the correct level for your zone.

▲ **Trim, defoliate, and mound up the bush with about 12 to 24 inches of soil and mulch. Tie up the canes, place the protective cone over the plant and weigh it down. Uncover after the last frost. Dieback should be pruned off.**

HOW TO PROTECT A ROSE BUSH

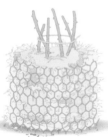

◀ **Using a collar of chicken wire, mound the rose bush with soil and mulch. Next, fill in the space between the canes with leaves, straw, and mulch. Any canes protruding from the chicken-wire collar may die back and can be removed during pruning. Remember, this is not necessary for areas in southern Zone 8 or higher.**

Hardy by nature

Hardiness is a measure of the ability of a rose to survive winter temperatures. (For more information on knowing a variety's hardiness see pages 66–67, "Roses in Your Climate," and the listings in the "Gallery of Roses.") How much protection you provide is governed by the severity of your winter cold and the hardiness of the rose you have selected. Many species roses, shrubs, old garden roses, and climbers, as well as some of the newer hybrid teas and floribundas, survive freezing and need little or no protection. Miniatures are more cold resistant than hybrid teas and need little protection (in Zone 6 and warmer areas, only 12 inches of dried leaves).

In areas where it rarely freezes, no winter protection is necessary. In any area where freezing is common, you'll need to protect roses that you're stretching out of their zone. Sometimes nature will do it for you. That first thick blanket of snow can be a good insulation if it stays in place. It keeps temperatures beneath it from dipping too far below freezing, but low enough to keep the plant in dormancy. Snow layers can also keep the canes from drying out in the wind.

ROSES HARDY TO ZONE 4

HYBRID TEAS
Brigadoon, Elina, Folklore, 'Fragrant Cloud', Ingrid Bergman, Kardinal, Lynn Anderson, Midas Touch, and Timeless

FLORIBUNDAS
'Betty Prior', Cherish, French Lace, Iceberg, Lavaglut, 'Little Darling', 'Permanent Wave', 'Playboy', Scentimental, and Sexy Rexy

SHRUBS
Most of the classic and modern shrubs in the Gallery of Roses (pages 106–115) are hardy to zone 4. The following are hardy to zone 3: 'Blanc Double de Coubert', Carefree Wonder, 'Frau Dagmar Hartopp', 'Hansa', *Rosa rugosa*, and 'Thérèse Bugnet'

OLD GARDEN ROSES
'Apothecary's Rose', Austrian Copper, 'Cardinal de Richelieu', 'Charles de Mills', 'Enfant de France', 'Ferdinand Pichard', 'La Belle Sultane', 'Rose de Meaux', 'Salet', and 'Superb Tuscan'

MINIATURES
Behold, Glowing Amber, Gourmet Popcorn, 'Green Ice', Little Artist, Minnie Pearl, Old Glory, and Roller Coaster

CLIMBING ROSES
Colette, Constance Spry, 'Dortmund', Dublin Bay, Eden, 'Jeanne Lajoie', 'Joseph's Coat', 'Lavender Lassie', 'New Dawn', 'Paul's Himalayan Musk Rambler', Polka, 'Prosperity', 'Sally Holmes', and 'William Baffin'

HOW TO PROTECT A CLIMBER

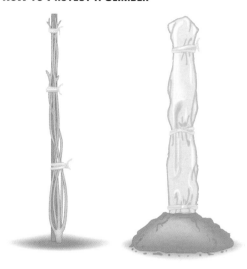

Providing extra protection

Many gardeners are unable to resist growing plants not rated to be hardy in their area. If you are one of those adventurers, you will need to provide special winter protection for your roses. In a cylinder made from chicken wire, cover the roses with about 12 inches of soil and an additional 12 inches of leaves (shredded oak leaves work well). This will protect the bud union and the lower portion of the canes. Remove the mound in spring and work it into the soil. You can also use rose cones made of polystyrene or compressed fiber. They're sold at garden centers in several sizes and should be filled with mounded soil and mulch. Weight them down with a brick. When the weather warms, remove the top (or cut the top off) to allow air circulation and to inhibit the growth of mold and fungi.

SUNPROOF AND RAINPROOF VARIETIES

These rose varieties are known for their stamina against strong sunlight and frequent rain showers.

HYBRID TEAS	FLORIBUNDAS	MINIATURES
Brandy	Amber Queen	Behold
Crystalline	Blueberry Hill	Carrot Top
Gold Medal	Dicky	Gourmet Popcorn
Ingrid Bergman	'Gene Boerner'	Miss Flippins
Perfect Moment	Iceberg	Old Glory
Signature	Nicole	Starina
Touch of Class	Playboy	

◀ **Trim, defoliate, and tie canes into a neat vertical bundle. Wrap the bundle with burlap, canvas, or a similar fabric (avoid plastic), and tie down for security. Mound the base of the plant with a mixture of mulch and soil.**

If you're growing climbers, untie them from their support, tie canes together in a bundle, and wrap them in burlap. To get tree roses through severe winters, partially dig them up, lay each on its side, and cover the horizontal plants with a mixture of soil and mulch.

When temperatures fall below 28°F, it's time to relocate your container roses. Move them to an unheated shelter or garage (but not colder than 10°F), away from the wind. When the foliage begins to fall, remove the remaining leaves completely. Water the plants occasionally, but hold off on fertilizing them. When all danger of spring frost is past, move the roses in their containers back outside. Prune them lightly to start new growth.

In areas where the temperature stays above 28°F (Zones 9 and 10), roses in containers can stay outside all winter. Remember to cut back on their water, and stop fertilizing them at all while they're dormant.

ROSES TOLERANT OF SHADE

These are the best roses for areas of the garden with less than six hours of sun per day.

FLORIBUNDAS	Roller Coaster
Betty Boop	Sweet Chariot
Blueberry Hill	
'Ivory Fashion'	SHRUBS
Playboy	Carefree Beauty
Playgirl	Carefree Delight
'Sweet Vivien'	Carefree Wonder
	'Erfurt'
MINIATURES	Flutterbye
'Green Ice'	'Gruss an Aachen'
Pinstripe	

HOW TO PROTECT A STANDARD TREE ROSE

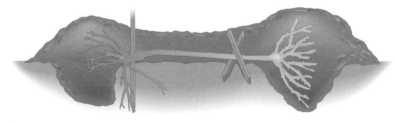

▲ **Trim and defoliate the bush, and partially uncover the root system to allow the tree to lie on its side. Secure the entire plant in place with crossed stakes, and cover it with a mixture of soil and mulch.**

PROTECTING FROM PESTS AND DISEASES

▶ **Knock Out is the first rose specifically bred for virtual immunity to black spot, a fungal disease that plagues roses throughout North America.**

Controlling diseases

Roses are susceptible to a variety of fungal, viral, and bacterial diseases whose effects can range from disfigurement of the leaves to outright killing of the plant. Because most diseases are hard to cure, it is usually easier to prevent them from taking hold in the first place.

Because well-maintained plants are less likely to succumb to diseases than weak ones, you can help ensure the health of your roses by caring for them properly. Follow the recommendations for watering (pages 42–43), fertilizing (pages 40–41), and pruning your roses (pages 44–49).

If you live where one or more rose diseases are common, you may wish to plant disease-resistant varieties.

Apart from practicing good garden hygiene and choosing disease-resistant plants, the best way to keep your roses from contracting diseases is to limit their exposure to the agents that spread them. Diseases are spread by air, water, and soil; by insects; and by direct contact with diseased plant material. Although you cannot completely protect your roses from these influences, you can at least exert some control over them. For instance, watering your roses by drip irrigation

rather than by an overhead method can help control black spot and other fungal diseases, which quickly grow under moist conditions. If you must water from above, do so in the morning to give leaves and flowers a chance to dry by nightfall. Applying a mulch prevents water from splashing onto plants from the ground during rain or irrigation and contaminating them with disease spores.

Good air circulation can also hold back mildew and other diseases by keeping plants dry and not allowing disease spores to take hold. To enhance air circulation, avoid planting your rose bushes too close together (see page 31 for spacing guidelines), and keep them from growing into one another if they become large. It also helps to keep the centers of the plants open through pruning.

Weeds can harbor many diseases, such as black spot and mildew, and disease-carrying insects, such as Japanese beetles and leafhoppers. You can eliminate this potential breeding ground by keeping weeds in check. If your garden has a large number of weeds, use a mulch or preemergence herbicide to control them. Insects known to be disease carriers can be eradicated with sprays or, if practical, picked from plants by hand or knocked off with a jet of water.

To keep diseases from spreading among your roses by direct contact, prune away and destroy diseased parts of plants. Pick up diseased leaves as soon as they fall.

Some diseases, such as crown gall, are soilborne. Many cannot be prevented or cured, so when a rose bush becomes infected, the only remedy is to replace both it and the surrounding soil. The diagnosis and treatment of specific diseases are described in The Ortho Rose Problem Solver, beginning on page 54.

Controlling insects and other pests

Hundreds of kinds of insects live in a typical garden, but only about a dozen regularly cause damage to roses. Indeed, some, such as ladybugs (also called lady beetles), are beneficial because they consume harmful insects. Although the variety of attackers is small, the damage the pests do can be extensive. Left unchecked in a rose garden, these insects can chew holes in leaves and flowers, suck vital juices from the plants, spread diseases, and even

▶ **Because weeds harbor many insects, controlling them is an important step toward controlling insect pests. Here's a good tip for pulling deep-rooted tree seedlings: Use a vise grip.**

kill the plants. Insect control is therefore essential to a healthy, productive rose garden.

As with diseases, the best way to reduce the chance of an insect attack is to practice good garden hygiene. Insects often live and lay eggs in weeds, so it is vital to keep the garden free of these breeding sites. Cleaning up garden debris as it accumulates and destroying it each fall so insects and their eggs cannot overwinter also reduce the insect threat. Even the tidiest garden can harbor destructive insects, so keep an eye out for initial signs of infestation. Catching a problem early can save your garden from serious damage.

Once you have identified an insect problem, you may choose to fight back with insecticides. Some insects, such as aphids, can be dislodged from plants by a jet of water, but insecticides are almost always a necessity at some time. Some products, such as insecticidal soaps and pyrethrin sprays, are biological. Synthetic formulations are usually stronger and longer lasting than organic agents and should be used with care around birds and pets.

Insecticides of either type are classed as contact or systemic. Contact insecticides are absorbed through the insects' bodies and must be sprayed onto them directly. Horticultural oil and insecticidal soap are types of contact insecticide that kill insects by smothering them or their eggs with a film. Systemic insecticides are applied to plants and taken up through their roots or leaves; insects are poisoned as they feast on plant parts. The type of insecticide you choose depends to a great extent on what works best in killing the insect that is causing the problem; see the recommendations on pages 54–59. Some insecticides, such as ORTHO Systemic Insect Killer, work both systemically and by contact.

In addition to insecticides, you may need to use miticides in your garden. These are formulated especially to control spider mites—tiny eight-legged relatives of spiders that disfigure leaves and flower buds with grayish webs. Like spiders, mites are not insects. Although some insecticides are effective against them, miticides are usually applied to kill them.

Insecticides and miticides are best used at the first sign of infestation. Spraying to prevent attack rarely works and is costly as well. It also can destroy natural predators and other beneficial insects. These products

◄ **A regular program of spraying prevents many diseases from gaining a foothold in your rose garden.**

can unnecessarily cause pests to build up an immunity so that these controls will not work when you need them.

Some rose growers prefer not to use any chemicals in their gardens and instead rely on natural predators to control destructive insects. Helpful species include ladybugs, assassin bugs, green lacewings, praying mantises, parasitic wasps, and predatory mites. The drawback to these insects is that, once they have eaten the pests in your garden, they will move on to other gardens in search of food. Their overall effectiveness may not last long.

SPRAYING TIPS

Before you use a sprayer for the first time, be sure to read the instructions accompanying it. Sprayers differ in design and operation, so it is important to follow the instructions carefully.

HERE ARE SOME GENERAL POINTERS:

■ Make sure plants are well watered before you spray, since damage is more likely to occur to dry leaves than to moist, turgid ones. Never spray on a windy day as too much spray will be blown away, perhaps onto plants that may be damaged by the product.

■ Spray both the upper and lower leaf surfaces until the spray starts to run off the leaf. Nozzles on some sprayers can be adjusted to produce different droplet sizes; the finer the spray, the more even the coverage.

■ When applying dormant sprays, make sure the canes are completely covered. Also cover the ground around the base of the plant.

■ When using a compression sprayer, you will need to repump occasionally to keep the pressure high enough to deliver a fine spray.

■ If the sprayer contains powdered material in suspension, you may need to shake it several times during spraying to keep the material evenly dispersed. Adding a squirt of liquid dish detergent to the water in the sprayer if powdered material is being used, either in suspension or in solution, helps it to adhere to the plants leaves. Liquid pesticide concentrates often contain a material that helps the active ingredient to adhere to the leaves, so liquid dish detergent is usually not necessary when using them.

■ When spraying a chemical that is toxic (the label will give this warning), wear a mask, gloves, and protective clothing. Change your clothes and take a shower as soon as you have finished the job.

■ Never apply insecticides or fungicides with a sprayer that has been used to apply weed killers. Residues of weed killer remaining in the sprayer can harm or kill your plants. To avoid this possibility, use a separate sprayer just for weed killers.

■ Keep your sprayer in good working order by cleaning and maintaining it properly. Nozzle apertures are small and clog easily. After each use, fill the sprayer with plain water and spray it through the nozzle to flush out any residue. If the nozzle becomes clogged, clean it by poking a thin wire through it. If you have a compression sprayer, you may need to apply a light oil to its pump cylinder from time to time to keep it working smoothly.

THE ORTHO ROSE PROBLEM SOLVER

Planting disease-resistant varieties that are hardy in your climate and keeping them vigorous with good gardening practices such as regular watering and feeding will increase your chances of enjoying healthy, colorful roses with few serious problems. Yet periods of drought and inattention are sometimes difficult to avoid, and they can pave the way for disease. Even the most disease-resistant rose can suffer damage from insects.

This section will help you solve the most common problems you might encounter with growing roses. It is based on The Ortho Problem Solver, a reference tool for solving plant problems. Here you will find the advice of many experts, most of them members of research universities and cooperative extension services.

To use the problem solver, select the picture that looks most like your problem. The map at the top shows how likely the problem is to affect your part of North America. If your region is red, the problem is common or severe. If it is yellow, the problem is occasional or moderate. If it is white, the problem is absent or minor.

The problem section describes the symptom or symptoms. The analysis section describes the organisms or cultural conditions causing the problem. The solution section tells you what you can do immediately to alleviate the problem. Then it tells you what changes you can make in the environment or in your gardening practices to prevent the problem from returning.

When you use chemical sprays make certain that roses are listed on the product label. Always read pesticide labels carefully and follow label directions to the letter.

For more information about the disease and insect controls recommended in this book, visit www.ortho.com.

Flower thrips

Flower thrips damage

Problem: Young leaves are distorted, and foliage may be flecked with yellow. Flower buds are deformed and usually fail to open. The petals of open blossoms, especially those of white or light-colored varieties, are often covered with brown streaks and red spots. If a deformed or streaked flower is pulled apart and shaken over white paper, tiny yellow or brown insects fall out.

Analysis: Flower thrips (*Frankliniella* spp.) live inside the buds and flowers of many garden plants, feeding on plant sap by rasping tissue. Injured petal tissue turns brown, and young leaves become deformed. Injured flower buds may fail to open. Thrips initially breed on grasses and weeds. When these begin to dry up or are harvested, the insects migrate to succulent green plants. Adults lay their eggs by inserting them into plant tissue. A complete life cycle may occur in 2 weeks, so populations build up rapidly. Most damage occurs in early summer.

Solution: Thrips are difficult to control because they continuously migrate to roses from other plants. Immediately remove and destroy infested buds and blooms. Spray with ORTHO Systemic Insect Killer, ORTHO Orthenex Insect & Disease Control, or ORTHO Bug-B-Gon Max Lawn and Garden Insect Killer three times at intervals of 7 to 10 days.

Rose midge

Rose midge damage

Problem: Buds are deformed, or black and crisp, and stem tips are dead. This condition develops rapidly. Tiny whitish maggots may be seen feeding at the base of buds or on the stem tips.

Analysis: The rose midge (*Dasineura rhodophaga*) is the larva of a tiny (1/20 inch), yellowish fly that appears in mid- or late summer. The females lay their eggs in growing tips, flower buds, and unfolding leaves, often 20 or 30 eggs to a bud. The eggs hatch in about two days, and the maggots feed, causing the tissue and buds to become distorted and blackened. When mature, the larvae drop to the ground to pupate. New adults appear in 5 to 7 days to lay more eggs. When infestations are severe, most or all of the buds and new shoots in an entire rose garden are killed.

Solution: Cut out and destroy infested stem tips and buds, and spray with ORTHO Rose & Flower Insect Killer. Repeat the spray if the plant becomes reinfested.

Black spot

Black spot

Problem: Circular black spots with fringed margins appear on the upper surface of the leaves in the spring. The tissue around the spots or the entire leaf may turn yellow, and the infected leaves may drop prematurely. Severely infected plants may lose all of their leaves by midsummer. Flower production is often reduced, and quality is poor.

Analysis: Black spot is caused by a fungus *(Diplocarpon rosae)* that is a severe problem in areas where high humidity or rain is common in spring and summer. The fungus spends the winter on infected leaves and canes. The spores are spread by splashing water and rain.

Solution: Spray with ORTHO RosePride Rose & Shrub Disease Control, ORTHO Orthenex Insect & Disease Control, or ORTHO Garden Disease Control. Repeat the treatment at intervals of 7 to 10 days for as long as the weather remains wet. Avoid overhead watering. During infestations and in the fall, rake up and destroy the fallen leaves. Resume spraying in spring. Plant resistant varieties.

Powdery mildew

Powdery mildew

Problem: Young leaves, young twigs, and flower buds are covered with a layer of grayish white powdery material. Leaves may be distorted and curled, and many may turn yellow or purplish and drop off. New growth is often stunted, and young canes may be killed. Badly infected flower buds do not open properly.

Analysis: Powdery mildew is a common plant disease caused by a fungus *(Sphaerotheca pannosa* var. *rosae)*. It is one of the most widespread and serious diseases of roses. The powdery covering consists of fungal strands and spores. The spores are spread by the wind to healthy plants. The fungus saps plant nutrients, causing distortion, discoloration, and often death of the leaves and canes. Powdery mildew may occur on roses anytime during the growing season when rainfall is low or absent, temperatures are between 70° and 80°F, nighttime relative humidity is high, and daytime relative humidity is low. Rose varieties differ in their susceptibility to powdery mildew.

Solution: Spray with ORTHO RosePride Rose & Shrub Disease Control, ORTHO Orthenex Insect & Disease Control, or ORTHO Garden Disease Control at the first sign of mildew. Repeat the spray at intervals of 7 to 10 days if mildew reappears. Rake and destroy leaves during infestations and in fall.

Rust

Rust

Problem: Yellow to brown spots, up to ¼ inch in diameter, appear on the upper surface of leaves, starting in spring or late fall. The lower leaves are affected first. On the underside are spots or blotches containing a red, orange, or black powdery material that can be scraped off. Infected leaves may become twisted and dry. Twigs may also be infected. Severely infected plants lack vigor.

Analysis: Rose rust is caused by any of several species of fungi *(Phragmidium* spp.) that infect only rose plants. Wind spreads the orange fungal spores to leaves. With moisture (rain, dew, or fog) and moderate temperatures (55° to 75°F), the spores enter the tissue on the underside of leaves. Spots develop on the upper surface. In the fall, black spores develop in the spots. These spores can survive the winter on dead leaves. In spring, the fungus produces the spores that cause new infections.

Solution: At the first sign, destroy the infected leaves and spray with ORTHO RosePride Rose & Shrub Disease Control, ORTHO Orthenex Insect & Disease Control, or ORTHO Garden Disease Control. Repeat every 7 to 14 days as long as conditions remain favorable for infection. During infestations and in fall, rake and destroy infected leaves and twigs. Plant resistant varieties.

Spider mites

Spider mite damage and webbing

Problem: Leaves are stippled, bronzed, and dirty. A silken webbing may be on the lower surface of the leaves or on new growth. Infested leaves often turn brown, curl, and drop off. Plants are usually weak. To determine if a plant is infested with mites, examine the leaf undersides with a hand lens. Or hold a sheet of white paper underneath an affected leaf and tap the leaf sharply. Minute specks the size of pepper grains will drop to the paper and begin to crawl around.
Analysis: Spider mites cause damage by sucking sap from the underside of leaves. The plant's green leaf pigment disappears, producing the stippled appearance. Spider mite webbing traps debris, making the plant messy. Many leaves may drop off. Severely infested plants produce few flowers. Mites are active throughout the growing season but thrive in hot, dry weather (70°F and above). By midsummer, they can build up to tremendous numbers.
Solution: Spray with ORTHO Systemic Insect Killer, ORTHO Rose and Flower Insect Killer, or ORTHO Bug-B-Gon MAX Garden & Landscape Insect Killer when damage is first noticed. Cover the underside of the leaves thoroughly. Repeat the application two more times every 7 to 10 days.

Leafhoppers

Damaged leaf. Inset: Leafhopper (2× life size)

Problem: Whitish insects, up to ½ inch long, hop and fly away quickly when the plant is touched. The leaves are stippled white. Severely infested plants may be killed.
Analysis: The rose leafhopper *(Edwardsiana rosae)* is a serious pest of roses and apples and infests several ornamental trees as well. It spends the winter as an egg, usually in pimplelike spots on rose canes or on apple bark. When the weather warms in the spring, young leafhoppers emerge and settle on the underside of leaves. They feed by sucking out the plant sap, which causes stippling of the leaves. The insects mature, and the females produce a second generation of leafhoppers. Eggs may be deposited in the leaf veins or leaf stems of the rose, or the leafhopper may fly to another woody plant to lay eggs. This second generation of leafhoppers feeds until fall. By feeding on the leaves and laying eggs in the rose canes, they may kill the plant.
Solution: Spray with ORTHO Systemic Insect Killer, ORTHO Rose and Flower Insect Killer, or ORTHO Bug-B-Gon MAX Garden & Landscape Insect Killer when damage is first noticed. Cover the lower surfaces of leaves thoroughly. Repeat the spray if the plant becomes reinfested.

Viruses

Virus disease

Problem: Yellow or brown rings, or yellow splotches of various sizes, appear on the leaves. The uninfected portions remain dark green. New leaves may be puckered and curling; flower buds may be malformed. Sometimes there are brown rings on the canes. The plants are usually stunted.
Analysis: Several viruses infect roses. The viruses are transmitted when an infected plant is grafted or budded to a healthy one. This generally occurs in the nursery. Some plants may show symptoms in only a few leaves. The virus is throughout the plant, however, and further symptoms may appear later. Most rose viruses are fairly harmless unless they cause extensive yellowing or browning. The virus suppresses the development of chlorophyll, causing the splotches or rings. Food production is reduced, which may result in stunted plant growth.
Solution: No cure is available for virus-infected plants. Rose viruses rarely spread naturally; therefore, only weak plants need to be removed. When purchasing rose bushes, buy only healthy plants from a reputable dealer. (For further information on selecting healthy plants, see pages 28–29.)

Rose aphid

Rose aphids (8× life size).

Problem: Tiny (⅛ inch) green or pink soft-bodied insects cluster on leaves, stems, and developing buds. When insects are numerous, flower buds are usually deformed and may fail to open properly. A shiny, sticky substance often coats the leaves. A black, sooty mold may grow on the sticky substance. Ants may be present.

Analysis: In small numbers the rose aphid (*Macrosiphum rosae*) does little damage. It is extremely prolific, however, and populations can rapidly build up to damaging levels during the growing season. Damage occurs when the aphid sucks the juices from rose stems and buds. It is unable to digest fully all the sugar in the plant sap and excretes the excess in a fluid called honeydew, which often drops onto the leaves below. A sooty mold fungus may develop on the honeydew, causing the rose plant to appear black and dirty. Ants feed on the sticky substance and are often present where there is an aphid infestation. When aphid populations are high, flower quality and quantity are reduced.

Solution: Spray with ORTHO Orthenex Insect & Disease Control, ORTHO Systemic Insect Killer, ORTHO Bug-B-Gon MAX Garden & Landscape Insect Killer, or an insecticidal soap when clusters of aphids are noticed. Repeat the treatment if the plant becomes reinfested.

Leafrollers

Rolled leaves

Problem: Leaves are rolled, usually lengthwise, and tied together with webbing. The rolled leaves are chewed, and the plant may be defoliated. When a rolled leaf is opened, a green caterpillar, ½ to ¾ inch long, may be found inside, surrounded by silky webbing. Flower buds also may be chewed.

Analysis: Several different leafrollers feed on rose leaves and buds. Leafrollers are the larvae of small (up to ¾ inch) brownish moths. The larvae feed on young foliage in the spring, sometimes tunneling into and mining the leaf first. They roll one to several leaves around themselves, tying them together with silken webbing. The rolled leaves provide protection from weather, parasites, and chemical sprays. Some leafrollers mature in summer and have several generations during the growing season, others only one a year.

Solution: Spray with ORTHO Systemic Insect Killer or the bacterial insecticide *Bacillus thuringiensis* (Bt) in the spring when leaf damage is first noticed. For the insecticide to be most effective, it should be applied before larvae are protected inside the rolled leaves. Check the plant periodically in spring for the first sign of infestation.

Caterpillars

Io caterpillar (life size)

Problem: Round or irregular holes appear in the leaves and buds. Leaves, buds, and flowers may be entirely chewed off. Caterpillars are found on the plant. Caterpillars are most active at night and can be present in large numbers.

Analysis: Caterpillars are the larvae of moths and butterflies. After hatching, the caterpillars eat leaves and flowers and develop into adults within a few weeks. Several generations of caterpillars are produced each year, primarily between early spring and late fall. The spines of some caterpillars (such as those of the Io caterpillar shown above) give a painful sting if touched.

Solution: Spray infested plants with ORTHO Systemic Insect Killer, ORTHO Rose and Flower Insect Killer, ORTHO Bug-B-Gon MAX Garden & Landscape Insect Killer, or with the bacterial insecticide *Bacillus thuringiensis* (Bt). If additional caterpillars are found, allow at least 7 days to pass between spray applications.

Rose slug

Rose slug (sawfly larvae, life size)

Problem: The surfaces of leaves are eaten between the veins; the translucent layer of tissue that remains turns brown. Later, large holes or the entire leaf, except the main vein, may be chewed. Pale green to metallic green sluglike worms, up to ¾ inch long, with large brown heads, may be found feeding on the leaves. Some have hairy bodies; others appear wet and slimy.

Analysis: Rose slugs are the larvae of black-and-yellow wasps called sawflies. The adult wasps appear in spring. They lay their eggs between the upper and lower surfaces of leaves along the leaf edges with a sawlike egg-laying organ. When the larvae emerge, they begin feeding on one surface of the leaf tissue, skeletonizing it. Later, several species of these larvae chew holes in the leaf or devour it entirely. When they are mature, the larvae drop to the ground, burrow into the soil, and construct cells in which to pass the winter. Some rose slugs pupate, emerge as sawflies, and repeat the cycle two to six times during the growing season. Infested roses may be weakened and produce few blooms.

Solution: Spray with ORTHO Systemic Insect Killer or ORTHO Bug-B-Gon MAX Garden & Landscape Insect Killer when damage is first noticed. Repeat if the rose becomes reinfested.

Scale insects

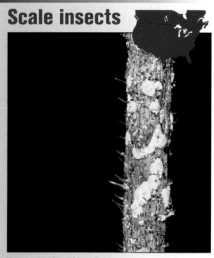

Rose scale (life size)

Problem: White, cottony masses; brown or black crusty bumps; or clusters of somewhat flattened white, yellowish, or brown scaly bumps cover the stems and leaves. The bumps can be scraped or picked off. Leaves turn yellow and may drop. In some cases, a shiny, sticky substance coats the leaves. A black, sooty mold often grows on the sticky substance. Heavy infestations kill the stems.

Analysis: Many types of scales infest roses. They lay eggs on leaves or canes, and in spring to midsummer the young crawlers settle on the leaves and twigs. These small (¹⁄₁₀ inch), soft-bodied young feed by sucking sap from the plant. The legs usually atrophy, and with some types, a shell develops over the body. Scales covered with a shell often blend in with the plant, and the eggs are inconspicuous beneath their covering. Scales that do not form a shell are conspicuous. Females of the cottony cushion scale are covered with a white, cottony egg sac containing as many as 2,500 eggs.

Solution: Control with ORTHO Systemic Insect Killer or ORTHO Rose and Flower Insect Killer when the young are active. To control overwintering insects, treat with ORTHO Volck Oil Spray in the spring.

Beetles

Japanese beetle. Inset: Fuller rose beetle

Problem: Holes appear in the flowers and flower buds; open flowers may be entirely eaten. Often affected buds fail to open, or they open deformed. Stem tips may be chewed, or the leaves may be notched or riddled with holes. Red, green-spotted, brownish, or metallic green beetles up to ½ inch long are sometimes seen on the flowers or foliage.

Analysis: Several different beetles infest roses. They may destroy the beauty of the plant by seriously damaging the flowers and foliage. The insects usually spend the winter as larvae in the soil or as adults in plant debris on the ground. In late spring or summer, mature beetles fly to roses and feed on the flowers, buds, and sometimes leaves. Punctured flower buds usually fail to open, and flowers that do open are often devoured. Many beetles feed at night, so their damage may be all that is noticed. Female beetles lay eggs in the soil or in flowers in late summer or fall. The larvae of some beetles feed on plant roots before maturing in the fall or spring.

Solution: Spray with ORTHO Systemic Insect Killer or ORTHO Bug-B-Gon MAX Garden & Landscape Insect Killer when damage is first noticed. Repeat if the rose becomes reinfested.

Crown gall

Crown gall

Problem: Large, corky galls up to several inches in diameter appear at the base of the plant and on the stems and roots. The galls are rounded, with a rough, irregular surface, and may be dark and cracked. Plants with numerous galls are weak; growth is slowed and leaves turn yellow. Branches or the entire plant may die back. Plants with only a few galls often show no other symptoms.

Analysis: Crown gall is a plant disease caused by a soil-inhabiting bacterium (*Agrobacterium tumefaciens*) that infects many ornamentals and fruit trees in the garden. The bacterium is often brought to a garden on the stems or roots of an infected plant and is spread with the soil and contaminated pruning tools. The galls may disrupt the flow of water and nutrients, weakening and stunting the top of the plant. Galls seldom cause the death of the plant.

Solution: Crown gall cannot be eliminated from a plant. An infected plant may survive for many years, however. To improve its appearance, prune out and destroy galled stems. Disinfect pruning shears after each cut. Destroy severely infected plants. The bacterium will remain in the soil for 2 to 3 years. If you wish to replace the infected roses soon, select plants that are resistant to crown gall.

Stem canker

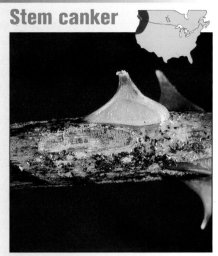

Stem cankers.

Problem: Yellowish, reddish, or brown sunken areas develop on canes. The sunken areas may have a purple margin, or they may be cracked. The leaves on affected canes are sometimes spotted, yellow, or wilting. Stems may die back.

Analysis: Several different fungi cause stem cankers on roses. During wet or humid weather, the fungi enter the plant at a wound caused by the thorns or at a cut stem. A sunken canker develops and expands through the tissue in all directions. The fungus may cut off the flow of nutrients and water through the stem, causing the leaves to wilt or yellow and the twigs to die back. Roses infected with black spot or in a weakened condition are more susceptible.

Solution: Cut out and destroy cankered canes at least 5 inches below the infected area. Disinfect pruning tools after each cut. After pruning, spray the canes with a fungicide containing lime sulfur. Sprays aimed at controlling black spot will help control canker. Repeat spraying every 10 to 14 days for as long as the weather is wet or humid. Keep the plants vigorous by feeding, watering, and pruning properly.

Borers

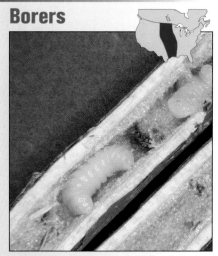

Carpenter bee larvae (3× life size).

Problem: Several or all of the larger canes and stems wilt and die. If the bark is peeled back, or if dying stems are sliced open, white to yellowish worms or legless grubs up to ¾ inch long may be revealed. Affected stems may be swollen at the base.

Analysis: Many kinds of insects bore into rose stems. They include certain sawflies, beetles, horntail wasps, and solitary bees. Some of these attack weakened plants or plants that are under stress from recent transplant or improper care; such borers often attack at the base of the plant. Other borers attack healthy rose plants, either traveling in a spiral pattern just under the bark or burrowing down through the center of the rose stems. Most rose borers produce one generation a year.

Solution: Prune out and destroy infested rose stems. Make the cut several inches below the point where the stem is wilted or swollen. If an insect has tunneled a hole through the center of the stem, keep cutting the stem lower to the ground until you find and destroy the insect or see the end of the tunnel. If this is a problem year after year, seal rose canes immediately after pruning with a sealer or with a thumbtack to prevent borers from penetrating the soft tissue in the center of the stem. Keep plants in good health.

ROSE CARE CALENDAR

ROSE CARE MONTH BY MONTH

HARDINESS ZONE	1	2	3	4	5	6	7	8	9	10	11
JANUARY											
Study catalogs; order roses	■	■	■	■	■	■	■	■	■	■	■
Clean and sharpen tools	■	■	■	■	■	■	■	■	■	■	■
Test pH; adjust if necessary								■	■	■	■
Plant container roses									■	■	■
Plant bare-root roses									■	■	■
Transplant roses									■	■	■
Prune roses									■	■	■
Fertilize after pruning									■	■	■
Resume watering as needed									■	■	■
Spray as needed									■	■	■
Weed rose beds; apply preemergence herbicide										■	■
February											
Study catalogs; order roses	■	■	■	■	■	■	■	■	■	■	■
Clean and sharpen tools	■	■	■	■	■	■	■	■			
Test pH; adjust if necessary								■			
Plant container roses								■	■	■	■
Plant bare-root roses								■	■	■	■
Transplant roses								■	■	■	■
Prune roses								■			
Fertilize after pruning								■			
Apply summer mulch									■	■	■
Water as needed									■	■	■
Spray as needed									■	■	■
Weed rose beds; apply preemergence herbicide								■	■		
March											
Study catalogs; order roses	■	■	■	■	■						
Clean and sharpen tools	■	■	■	■	■						
Test pH; adjust if necessary						■	■				
Plant container roses						■	■	■	■	■	■
Plant bare-root roses						■	■				
Transplant roses						■	■				
Remove winter protection						■					
Prune roses						■					
Fertilize after pruning						■					
Fertilize roses								■	■	■	■
Apply supplemental liquid fertilizer								■	■	■	■
Weed rose beds						■					
Weed rose beds; apply preemergence herbicide								■	■	■	■
Apply summer mulch								■			
Begin regular spraying								■			
Continue regular spraying									■	■	■
Water as needed								■	■	■	■
Disbud for larger flowers								■	■	■	■
Deadhead faded flowers									■	■	■

Rose Care Month by Month

Hardiness Zone	1	2	3	4	5	6	7	8	9	10	11
April											
Test pH; adjust if necessary	■	■	■	■	■	■	■				
Plant container roses	■	■	■	■	■	■	■	■	■	■	■
Plant bare-root roses	■	■	■	■	■	■	■				
Transplant roses	■	■	■	■	■	■	■				
Remove winter protection	■	■	■	■	■	■	■				
Prune roses	■	■	■	■	■	■	■				
Fertilize after pruning	■	■	■	■	■	■	■				
Fertilize roses								■	■	■	■
Apply supplemental liquid fertilizer					■	■	■	■	■	■	
Weed rose beds			■	■	■	■	■				
Weed rose beds; apply preemergence herbicide			■	■	■		■				
Apply summer mulch								■			
Continue regular spraying								■	■	■	■
Water as needed								■	■	■	■
Disbud for larger flowers								■	■	■	■
Deadhead faded flowers								■	■	■	■
May											
Plant container roses	■	■	■	■	■	■	■	■	■	■	■
Plant bare-root roses	■	■	■	■							
Fertilize roses	■	■	■	■	■	■	■	■	■	■	■
Apply supplemental liquid fertilizer	■	■	■	■	■	■	■	■	■	■	
Weed rose beds	■	■	■	■	■	■	■	■	■	■	■
Weed; apply preemergence herbicide	■	■									
Apply summer mulch	■	■	■	■	■	■	■				
Begin regular spraying	■	■	■	■	■	■	■				
Continue regular spraying								■	■	■	■
Water as needed	■	■	■	■	■	■	■	■	■	■	■
Disbud for larger flowers	■	■	■	■	■	■	■	■	■	■	■
Deadhead faded flowers								■	■	■	■
June											
Plant container roses	■	■	■	■	■	■	■	■	■	■	■
Fertilize roses	■	■	■	■	■	■	■	■	■	■	■
Apply supplemental liquid fertilizer	■	■	■	■	■	■	■	■	■	■	■
Weed rose beds	■	■	■	■	■	■	■	■	■	■	
Apply summer mulch	■	■	■	■							
Continue regular spraying	■	■	■	■	■	■	■	■	■	■	■
Water as needed	■	■	■	■	■	■	■	■	■	■	■
Disbud for larger flowers	■	■	■	■	■	■	■	■	■	■	■
Deadhead faded flowers	■	■	■	■	■	■	■	■	■	■	■

ROSE CARE MONTH BY MONTH

Hardiness Zone	1	2	3	4	5	6	7	8	9	10	11
July											
Plant container roses	■	■	■	■	■	■	■	■	■	■	■
Fertilize roses	■	■	■	■	■	■	■	■	■	■	■
Apply supplemental liquid fertilizer	■	■	■	■	■	■	■	■	■	■	■
Weed rose beds	■	■	■	■	■	■	■	■	■	■	■
Continue regular spraying	■	■	■	■	■	■	■	■	■	■	■
Water as needed	■	■	■	■	■	■	■	■	■	■	■
Disbud for larger flowers	■	■	■	■	■	■	■	■	■	■	■
Deadhead faded flowers	■	■	■	■	■	■	■	■	■	■	■
August											
Plant container roses	■	■	■	■	■	■	■	■	■	■	■
Fertilize roses								■	■	■	■
Apply supplemental liquid fertilizer	■	■	■	■	■	■	■	■	■	■	■
Apply fertilizer for the last time	■	■	■	■	■	■	■				
Weed rose beds	■	■	■	■	■	■	■	■	■	■	■
Continue regular spraying	■	■	■	■	■	■	■	■	■	■	■
Water as needed	■	■	■	■	■	■	■	■	■	■	■
Disbud for larger flowers	■	■	■	■	■	■	■	■	■	■	■
Deadhead faded flowers	■	■	■	■	■	■	■	■	■	■	■
September											
Order roses for fall planting							■	■	■	■	■	■
Prepare soil for spring planting	■	■	■	■	■						
Plant container roses							■	■	■	■	■	■
Apply fertilizer for the last time								■	■	■	■
Weed rose beds					■	■	■	■	■	■	■
Continue regular spraying							■	■	■	■	■
Water as needed					■	■	■	■	■	■	■
Stop deadheading roses	■	■	■	■	■	■					

ROSE CARE MONTH BY MONTH

Hardiness Zone	1	2	3	4	5	6	7	8	9	10	11
October											
Apply winter protection	■	■	■	■							
Order roses for fall planting						■	■	■	■	■	■
Prepare soil for spring planting					■						
Plant container roses						■	■	■	■	■	
Transplant roses					■						
Weed rose beds						■	■	■	■	■	■
Continue regular spraying							■	■	■	■	■
Water as needed					■	■	■	■	■	■	■
Stop deadheading roses							■	■	■	■	■
November											
Apply winter protection					■	■	■				
Order roses for spring planting	■	■	■	■	■	■	■	■	■	■	■
Prepare soil for spring planting						■	■	■	■	■	■
Plant container roses								■	■	■	■
Plant bare-root roses						■	■	■	■	■	■
Transplant roses						■	■	■			
Spray as needed									■	■	■
Withhold water from established plants									■	■	■
December											
Order roses for spring planting	■	■	■	■	■	■	■	■	■	■	■
Prepare soil for spring planting								■	■	■	■
Plant container roses								■	■	■	■
Plant bare-root roses								■	■	■	■
Transplant roses								■	■	■	■
Spray as needed									■	■	■

GALLERY OF ROSES

Using this guide

When you plant roses in your garden they will repay you with beauty and fragrance for many years to come. But which roses should you plant? The selections in this guide will help you answer that question. Here you will find described and illustrated more than 350 roses from the more than 20,000 cultivars currently available. They were chosen based on these factors: ease of availability coast to coast; vigor, disease resistance, and hardiness; fragrance, variety of color and shape; and ratings in nationwide evaluations. The selections are alphabetized within use categories that have been modified from the rose group classifications of the American Rose Society. "In This Section" at left gives you a complete picture of these categories and where to find them.

Of course, any list will be, at least in part, subjective. The roses in this guide undeniably represent favorites. You may find it rewarding to experiment with other roses you find at garden centers and plant sales—there are literally thousands to learn about and to enjoy.

Making selections

Each rose listing includes a photograph and certain standard information. The varietal names are the ones most likely to be encountered in nurseries and catalogs (see "What's In a Name?" on page 7). Capitalized names enclosed in single quotation marks are officially registered cultivar names. Initial-capped names not enclosed in single quotation marks are commercial names, many of which are trademarked or registered. Each time a rose is listed in this gallery, its name is followed by its classification (see pages 12–13), color category (see pages 10–11), introducer or breeder, year of introduction, notes on special features (including regional notes and number of petals as a gauge of

◀ **The floribunda rose, Julia Child**

blossom fullness), USDA Hardiness Zone, and, if applicable, its Roses in Review (RIR) rating and important awards (see below for a description of each award and the abbreviations used in this gallery). The zones listed are from the USDA Plant Hardiness Zone Map on pages 66–67. There you will also find abbreviations that indicate sections of the country within hardiness zones in which the selection will thrive. The sizes listed are the average for that variety under optimum conditions.

Roses in Review (RIR)

This is a rating given to a rose after a three-year evaluation by growers from all regions of the country in the American Rose Society's Roses in Review program. The ratings translate as follows:

- **9.3–10:** One of the best roses ever.
- **8.8–9.2:** An outstanding rose.
- **8.3–8.7:** A very good to excellent rose.
- **7.8–8.2:** A solid to very good rose.
- **7.3–7.7:** A good rose.
- **6.8–7.2:** An average rose.
- **6.1–6.7:** A below-average rose.
- **6.0 or less:** Not recommended.

Not all roses have an RIR rating; some are too new to have completed their evaluation, and some older roses were not evaluated when the program began more than 20 years ago. Keep in mind that this rating is only an average of a number of characteristics important to gardeners, as well as an average of a variety's performance over the entire country. A rose may have a relatively low RIR rating, yet still be an outstanding performer in a more limited geographical area or possess other desirable characteristics. If you are attracted to a low-rated rose, try it. It may perform surprisingly well in your garden.

With this information, you can make selections that are specific to your garden and appealing to your tastes. If you're a beginning rose gardener, this guide will get you started. But even if you're an experienced rose gardener, you'll find some exciting new treasures to enjoy.

THE MAJOR AWARDS

WORLD FEDERATION OF ROSE SOCIETIES AWARDS:

World's Favorite Rose–Hall of Fame (WFRS/HOF) Every three years a ballot is taken for this prestigious award by the 37-member national rose societies belonging to the World Federation of Rose Societies. So far only 13 roses have received it.

WFRS Old Garden Rose Hall of Fame (WFRS/OGR) In 1988 at the World Rose Convention in Sydney, Australia, members decided to establish an Old Rose Hall of Fame to recognize roses of historical or genealogical importance and roses that have enjoyed continued popularity over a great many years.

AMERICAN ROSE SOCIETY AWARDS

American Rose Society Award of Excellence (ARS/AOE) The popularity of miniature roses led to this award in 1975. Miniature roses are evaluated over two years in seven test gardens by teams of ARS members. The elements evaluated include novelty, bud form, flower form, color opening, color finishing, substance, habit, quantity of flowers, vigor/renewal, foliage, and pest resistance.

American Rose Society Miniature Rose Hall of Fame (ARS/HOF) To further promote miniature roses, the ARS Miniature Hall of Fame was established in 1998. Nominations are solicited from ARS members each spring with only varieties in commerce for more than 20 years qualifying for consideration.

American Rose Society James Alexander Gamble Fragrance Medal (ARS/GFM) This medal is awarded to outstanding roses with exceptional fragrance. The selection is made after a five-year evaluation by the ARS Prizes and Awards Committee. The rose must be registered and must have an RIR rating of at least 7.5. It is not mandatory that a rose be selected yearly for this medal.

ALL-AMERICA ROSE SELECTION AWARD

All-America Rose Selection (AARS) All-America Rose Selections (AARS) is a nonprofit association of commercial rose growers and introducers organized to promote exceptional roses. Since 1938 the coveted AARS seal has been awarded each year to only a few outstanding new rose varieties. Evaluation consists of an extensive two-year trial program in 27 test gardens throughout the country representing different climate zones. AARS evaluates roses on various criteria: vigor, fragrance, disease resistance, foliage, flower production, growth habit, bud and flower form, opening and finishing color, and stem.

INTERNATIONAL ROSE TRIAL AWARDS

PORTLAND'S BEST ROSE (PBR), PORTLAND GOLD MEDAL (PGM), ROSE HILLS GOLDEN ROSE (RHGR), ROSE HILLS GOLD MEDAL (RHGM) To date more than 30 international rose trials are conducted throughout the world. Two such trials exist in the United States—the International Rose Test Garden at Washington Park in Portland, Oregon, and the International Rose Trial Garden at The Rose Hills Company in Whittier, California.

Varieties are judged throughout a two-year period. The permanent judging panel during each scheduled site inspection scores based on the following criteria: novelty, bud and flower form, color opening, color finishing, substance, habit, quantity of flowers, vigor/renewal, foliage, disease/insect resistance, and fragrance. At the end of the evaluation period, the rose receiving the most points is given a special prize (PBR and RHGR), and the top varieties in each classification receive a Gold Medal (PGM and RHGM).

Roses and Your Climate

Calgary

Vancouver
Pacific Northwest (PNW)

Regina

Seattle

Portland

Bozeman

Idaho Falls

Casper

San
Francisco

Salt Lake
City

Denver

Las Vegas

Los
Angeles

Albuquerque

Pacific Southwest (PSW)

North Central (NC)

Winnipeg

Bismarck

Rapid City

Minneapolis

Milwaukee

Detroit

Des Moines

Chicago

Omaha

Indianapolis

Kansas City

St. Louis

Wichita

Louisville

Oklahoma
City

Little Rock

Memphis

Dallas

Jackson

San Antonio

Houston

New
Orleans

South Central (SC)

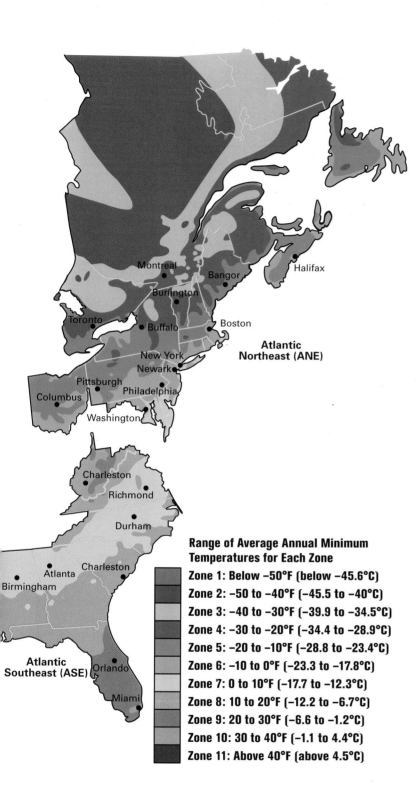

Range of Average Annual Minimum Temperatures for Each Zone

Zone 1: Below –50°F (below –45.6°C)

Zone 2: –50 to –40°F (–45.5 to –40°C)

Zone 3: –40 to –30°F (–39.9 to –34.5°C)

Zone 4: –30 to –20°F (–34.4 to –28.9°C)

Zone 5: –20 to –10°F (–28.8 to –23.4°C)

Zone 6: –10 to 0°F (–23.3 to –17.8°C)

Zone 7: 0 to 10°F (–17.7 to –12.3°C)

Zone 8: 10 to 20°F (–12.2 to –6.7°C)

Zone 9: 20 to 30°F (–6.6 to –1.2°C)

Zone 10: 30 to 40°F (–1.1 to 4.4°C)

Zone 11: Above 40°F (above 4.5°C)

Most roses are too tender for their aboveground growth to survive deep freezes. It is important to select roses that are proven performers in your climate. Some varieties require protection during cold winters, but they will survive mild winters quite easily. In areas where temperatures drop below 20°F, provide some measure of protection for most roses (see "Protection from the Elements," pages 50–51). Still, many modern roses survive mild winter climates without any protection. If your climate is colder, consider hardy old garden roses as well as shrub roses—or provide increased winter protection.

The hardiest roses are centifolias, albas, gallicas, and rugosas, all of which tolerate temperatures as low as –30° F with little damage to aboveground growth.

How to locate your hardiness zone

The USDA Agricultural Research Service climate map describes the normal average annual minimum temperature zones for the United States and Canada. For instance, in Chicago the USDA Hardiness Zone is 5—meaning the temperature hits an average low during the winter months of –10°F to –20°F. In general, rose growers who live in or near Zone 6 or colder areas need to select roses that are not tender and provide some measure of winter protection. In Zone 8 and warmer locales, no protection is needed except perhaps against sun, high temperatures, and strong winds.

Regional weather zones

In addition to hardiness zones, consider your region when selecting roses. Some varieties flourish in certain regions and underperform in others because of specific climatic conditions in a particular area. The map at left divides much of North America into six regions: Atlantic Northeast (ANE), Atlantic Southeast (ASE), North Central (NC), South Central (SC), Pacific Northwest (PNW), and Pacific Southwest (PSW). For example, a variety may perform well in Seattle (PNW) and not so well in Dallas (SC), even though they're both in USDA Zone 5. This guide lists which of the six regional areas are recommended for a rose, if it applies.

HYBRID TEAS AND GRANDIFLORAS

These are the long-stemmed roses you give (and receive) on Valentine's Day. Their cherished, perfectly pointed buds open to nodding but elegant blooms of just about every conceivable color in the rainbow. This is the most popular class of modern roses, with each bloom containing 25 to 50 petals on a long stem, either singly or with several side buds. Plants are available in both bush and standard tree forms.

The introduction of 'Peace' in 1945 heralded the modern era of the hybrid tea. It was overwhelmingly accepted and praised, and hybrid teas attained a zenith of symmetrical beauty. Recent All-America Rose Selections (AARS) in the hybrid tea class have been Tahitian Sunset, Whisper, Love and Peace, Gemini, Elle, and Glowing Peace.

In 1954, Walter Lammerts crossed the hybrid tea 'Charlotte Armstrong' with the floribunda 'Floradora', resulting in a carmine rose and dawn pink variety with the characteristics of a hybrid tea and the ability to bear clusters of flowers and grow to a commanding height of 6 to 8 feet or more—and the class called grandiflora was born. 'Queen Elizabeth' was the first member of this class. Other popular varieties include Wild Blue Yonder, Strike it Rich, Crimson Bouquet, and About Face.

About Face ('WEKosupalz'). Gr, ob, Carruth, 2005. Tall, upright bush with medium to large fully double blooms that are apple scented. The plant is clean, with superb vigor and good repeat. About 35 petals. Zones 5 to 10.
Awards: AARS 2005

Aromatherapy ('JAChonew'). HT, mp, Zary, 2005. Strong and upright grower producing a great number of blooms all season. Long lasting and excellent for cutting with an overwhelming fruity fragrance. About 30 petals. Zones 5 to 10.

Barbra Streisand ('WEKquaneze'). HT, m, Carruth, 2004. Rich lavender blooms show off beautifully against shiny dark green foliage. Blooms are heavily scented on long, strong stems that are excellent for cutting. 25 to 30 petals. Zones 5 to 11. RIR= 7.1
Awards: RHGM 2004

'Anastasia'. HT, w, Greff, 1980. Magnificent exhibition-form blooms borne singly on long, strong stem. Vigorous and dense grower, the bush is clean and quite prolific. 30 petals. Zones 5 to 10. RIR=7.3

Betty White ('MEIceppus'). HT, pb, Meilland, 2004. Large flowers with old-fashioned form, delightful light pink outer petals and apricot tones blending at the center. Good-quality blooms with strong, classic rose fragrance. 60 to 65 petals. Zones 5 to 10.

Brandy ('AROcad'). HT, ab., Swim & Christensen, 1981. Rich mahogany-tinted foliage. Plant is tender and requires protection in winter. Spicy fragrance. 25 to 30 petals. Zones 6 to 11. RIR=7.4
Awards: AARS 1982

Bride's Dream ('KORoyness'). HT, lp, Kordes, 1985. Lovely pale pink flowers, borne singly and profusely throughout the season, long lasting with magnificent high-centered form. 25 to 30 petals. Zones 5 to 10. RIR= 8.1

Black Magic ('TANkalgic'). HT, dr, Tantau, 1997. Really dark red blooms on a medium to tall, vigorous bush, extremely long-lasting blooms are superb for cutting and exhibition. About 30 petals. Zones 5 to 10. RIR= 7.7

Brigadoon ('JACpal'). HT, pb, Warriner, 1992. Changes color as it opens from bud to bloom, vigorous, dark green foliage that can be quite large in cooler climates. 25 to 30 petals. Zones 4 to 9. RIR=7.8
Awards: AARS 1992

Cabana ('JACepirt'). HT, pb, Zary, 2000. Eyecatching blooms, 5 1/2 inches across, with rose, pink, and yellow stripes. The bush is tall and the long, strong stems are ideal for cutting. 25 to 30 petals. Zones 7 to 11. RIR= 7.6

Chris Evert ('WEKjuvoo'). HT, ob, Carruth, 1997. Spectacular color and long-lasting blooms that will surely attract a lot of attention in any garden. Good vigor, clean, and repeats well. 25 to 30 petals. Zones 5 to 11. RIR=7.5

'Chrysler Imperial'. HT, dr, Lammerts, 1952. Rich velvety blooms with a powerful fragrance. Prone to mildew. Likes the heat in ASE, SC, and PSW. 45 to 50 petals. Zones 5 to 10. RIR=7.8
Awards: AARS 1953, ARS/GFM 1965, PGM 1951

Crimson Bouquet ('KORbeteilich'). Gr, dr, Kordes, 2000). Blooms come singly and in clusters on a medium, upright bushy bush with dark green glossy foliage that is disease resistant. 20 to 25 petals; Zones 6 to 10. RIR=7.9
Awards: AARS 2000, PBR

Diana, Princess of Wales ('JACshaq'). HT, pb, Zary, 1999. A beautiful rose worthy of its namesake, graced with impeccable form, sweet fragrance of tea. Tall, vigorous, and clean plant. 26 to 40 petals. Zones 5 to 11. RIR=7.5

Double Delight ('ANDeli'). HT, rb, Swim & Ellis, 1977. Most popular rose of last 30 years; vigorous, beautiful foliage; requires sun to develop full red color; prone to mildew without protection; spicy fragrance. 30 to 35 petals. Zones 6 to 10. RIR=8.4
Awards: AARS 1977, WFRS/HOF 1985, ARS/GFM

'Duet'. HT, mp, Swim, 1960. Classic variety and after nearly half a century still popular among rose growers for its delicate beauty and long-lasting quality. 25 to 30 petals. Zones 6 to 11. RIR=6.8
Awards: AARS 1961, RHGM 2004

Elina ('DICjana'). HT, ly, Dickson, 1984. Tall and vigorous with loads of blossoms all summer and into fall. Very light fragrance. 30 to 35 petals. Zones 4 to 11. RIR=8.6
Awards: WFRS/HOF 2006, PGM 1996

'Elizabeth Taylor'. HT, dp, Weddle 1985. Shocking color with smoky edges, prefers moderate to warm climates for best size, light fragrance. 30 to 35 petals. Zones 5 to 10. RIR=8.4

Elle ('MEIbderos'). HT, op, Meilland, 2005. A variety that will surely attract a lot of attention in your garden for its ability to bloom profusely; easy to grow and maintain. 41+ petals. Zones 6 to 11. **Awards:** AARS 2005

Fragrant Cloud ('TANellis'). HT, or, Tantau, 1963. Strong, spicy-sweet fragrance; vigorous, dark glossy foliage; responds well to harsh pruning after winter. 25 to 30 petals. Zones 6 to 11. RIR=8.1 **Awards:** PGM 1966, ARS/GFM 1970, WFRS/HOF 1981

Gemini ('JACnepal'). HT, pb, Zary 2000. ARS members favorite rose for 2005. Exhibitors love the impeccable form, long strong stems, and foliage; gardeners love it for the color, abundant bloom and easy care. 25 to 30 petals. Zones 6 to 11. RIR=8.2 **Awards:** AARS 2000, RHGM 2003, PBR 2003

Gift of Life ('HARelan'). HT, yb, Harkness, 1999. Excellent variety for home gardeners who want their roses to bloom constantly and almost nonstop. Vigorous, well behaved, and clean. 26 to 40 petals. Zones 6 to 10. RIR=7.6 **Awards:** PBR

Glowing Peace ('MEIzoelo'). Gr, yb, Meilland, 2000. A boldly colored version of the world-famous 'Peace', with the same growing habit and vigor. 26 to 40 petals. Zones 6 to 10. RIR=7.4 **Awards:** AARS 2001

Gold Medal ('AROyqueli'). Gr, my, Christensen, 1982. Weatherproof blossoms, tall, very vigorous. Color is deeper in moderate climates; best in PSW, SC, and ASE. 30 to 35 petals. Zones 5 to 10. RIR=8.4

Grand Finale ('JACpihi'). HT, w, Zary, 1998. Long, pointed buds open to magnificent blooms with high center and honeysuckle fragrance. Bloom size is about 4½ inches, and the stems are long. 30 petals. Zones 6 to 10. RIR=7.4

'Great Scott'. HT, mp, Ballin, 1990. Tall bush with a tendency to spread. Large flowers, fully double with tremendous substance, open slowly to show their lovely form. 30 to 40 petals. Zones 6 to 11. RIR=7.7

Honey Dijon ('WEKsproulses'). Gr, r, Sproul, 2005. An unusual color beloved by many, especially flower arrangers. 25 to 30 petals. Zones 5 to 10.

Honor ('JAColite'). HT, w, Warriner, 1980. Stately looking; foliage is large and dark green, with good disease resistance; stems tend to be too long at times. Best in cooler coastal regions, especially PNW. 25 to 30 petals. Zones 6 to 10. RIR=7.6
Awards: AARS 1980, PGM 1978

Ingrid Bergman ('POUlman'). HT, dr, Poulsen 1984. Long, straight stems and deep green, disease-resistant foliage. Tends to grow taller than other hybrid teas. Hardy, but a little heat improves flower color. 35 to 40 petals. Zones 6 to 11. RIR=7.8
Awards: WFRS/HOF 2000

'Jane Pauley'. HT, ob, Weddle, 1992. Large, exhibition-type blooms up to 6½ inches across, borne singly with moderate fragrance. Vigorous and upright. 35 petals. Zones 6 to 10. RIR=7.2.

'Janice Kellogg'. F, dp, Meilland, 2006. Medium height, bushy habit. Blooms are large and truly multipetaled with old-fashioned form and old rose scent. 60+ petals. Zones 5 to 10.

'John F. Kennedy'. HT, w, Boerner, 1965. Blooms are tough enough to survive cold or heat, but production can be disappointing; moderate licorice fragrance. 40 to 50 petals. Zones 6 to 10. RIR=6.3

'Just Joey'. HT, ob, Cants, 1972. Large ruffled flowers last for weeks with good color, fruity fragrance. Vigorous and moderately hardy. 25 to 30 petals. Zones 6 to 10. RIR=7.9
Awards: WFRS/HOF 1994

Kardinal ('KORlingo'). HT, mr, Kordes, 1986. Originally bred for the cut flower industry; small, perfect flower form; outstanding in PNW. Vigorous grower. 30 to 35 petals. Zones 6 to 11. RIR=8.5

Let Freedom Ring ('WEKearman'). HT, mr, Earman, 2006. New variety is slowly gaining a following among exhibitors and home gardeners alike. Impeccable form, long-lasting blooms on long stems. 25 petals. Zones 5 to 10.

'Louise Estes'. HT, pb, Winchell, 1991. Blooms ruffled at edges in cool climates; vigorous-growing, tall, upright bush; resistant to mildew. Fruity fragrance. 40 to 45 petals. Zones 5 to 10. RIR=8.3

Love and Peace ('BAIpeace'). HT, yb, Twomey & Lim, 2002. Constant bloomer, and there will still be plenty of flowers left after you've made a bouquet to bring indoors. 40+ petals. Zones 6 to 10. RIR=7.7
Awards: AARS 2002

Marilyn Monroe ('WEKsunspat'). HT, ab, Carruth, 2002. Lovely and fitting tribute to the legendary film star; impeccable form; long lasting blooms with long, strong stems; excellent for exhibition or cutting; very thorny. 30 to 35 petals. Zones 5 to 10. RIR=7.8

Memorial Day ('WEKblunez'). HT, mp, Carruth, 2004. Enormous blooms look old-fashioned and have a strong classic old rose fragrance. Vigorous, upright, and disease free. 50+ petals. Zones 6 to 10.
Awards: AARS 2004

Midas Touch ('JACtou'). HT, dy, Christensen, 1992. Color holds, but isn't weatherproof— blooms can open too fast in warmer climates. Prolific and disease resistant. 20 to 25 petals. Zones 6 to 11. RIR=7.5
Awards: AARS 1994

'Mikado'. HT, rb, Suzuki, 1987. Highly polished, medium green foliage; two-toned blooms with light, spicy fragrance intensify in color in spring and fall. 30 to 35 petals. Zones 5 to 10. RIR=7.4
Awards: AARS 1988

'Mister Lincoln'. HT, dr, Swim & Weeks, 1964. Tall, vigorous, subject to infection by mildew and black spot if unprotected. Heavy damask fragrance. Best where days are warm and nights cool: PSW and SC. 30 to 35 petals. Zones 5 to 10. RIR=8.3
Awards: AARS 1965, ARS/GFM 2003

Moonstone ('WEKcryland'). HT, w, Carruth, 1998. A top exhibition rose and still gaining a lot of following for the beauty and form of its flowers and their lasting quality when brought indoors. 30 to 35 petals. Zones 6 to 11. RIR=8.2
Awards: RHGM 2002

Neptune ('WEKhilpurnil'). HT, m, Carruth, 2005. Produces abundant blooms with good form and powerfully sweet fragrance all season long. Medium growing, upright, and bushy. 26 to 40 petals. Zones 5 to 10.

New Zealand ('MACgenev'). HT, lp, McGredy, 1991. Blooms have great substance and form, strong honeysuckle fragrance; size best in cooler climates. 30 to 35 petals. Zones 6 to 10. RIR=7.9
Awards: PBR 1985

Olympiad ('MACauck'). HT, mr, McGredy, 1982. Host of blossoms on a healthy, easy-to-grow bush. Large foliage is deeply veined; disease resistant. 35 petals. Zones 6 to 10. RIR=8.6
Awards: AARS 1984. PBR

Opening Night ('JAColber'). HT, rb, Zary, 1998. Simply sparkles. Strong, straight stems and dark green, disease-free foliage. Prefers cooler temperatures. 25 to 30 petals. Zones 5 to 10. RIR=7.8
Awards: AARS 1998

Papa Meilland ('MEIsar'). HT, dr, Meilland, 1963. Pointed buds open to high-centered, multipetaled blooms with an overpowering scent. One of the best in its color class after nearly a half century. 35 petals. Zones 6 to 10. RIR=7.8
Awards: WFRS/HOF 1988, ARS/GFM 1974

Pascali ('LENip'). HT, w, Lens, 1963. Classic variety still widely grown, especially in public gardens. Winner of numerous gold medals at various rose trials. 30 petals. Zones 6 to 10. RIR=7.8
Awards: AARS 1969, WFRS/HOF 1991, PGM 1967

'Peace'. HT, yb, Meilland 1945. Established the hybrid-tea standards in the 20th century. Opulent blossoms, foliage is large, glossy green, easy to grow, very fragrant. Color is best east of the Rockies in NC and SC. 40 to 45 petals. Zones 5 to 9. RIR=8.1
Awards: AARS 1946, WFRS/HOF 1976, PGM 1944

Perfect Moment ('KORwilma'). HT, rb, Kordes 1989. Large weather-proof, long-lasting blooms, compact bush with dark green leaves, disease resistant, moderate summer temperatures give brightest colors. 25 to 30 petals. Prone to mildew. Zones 5 to 10. RIR=7.8.
Awards: AARS 1991

Peter Mayle ('MEIzincaro'). HT, dp, Meilland, 2003. Extremely vigorous bush that can survive the heat and humidity of summer. Lovely blooms with good form and a strong old rose fragrance that you can enjoy in the garden and indoors. 30 to 35 petals. Zones 6 to 10. RIR=7.7

Pope John Paul II ('JACsegra'). HT, w, Zary, 2007. A new rose that has earned high marks in test gardens for vigor, disease resistance, generosity of bloom, and flower form. It also has a lovely citrus fragrance. 50 petals. Zones 5 to 11.

Pristine ('JACpico'). HT, w, Warriner, 1978. Large, substantial blossoms on strong, thorny stems open fast but last only a few days. The thick foliage is disease free. 25 to 30 petals. Zones 6 to 10. RIR=8.6
Awards: PGM 1979

'Queen Elizabeth'. Gr, mp, Lammerts, 1954. Considered the first grandiflora. Large trusses of blooms on strong, straight stems. Color is clear, weatherproof in any climate. A climbing version exists. 35 petals. Zones 5 to 10. RIR=7.8
Awards: AARS 1955, WFRS/HOF 1979, PGM 1954

Ronald Reagan Rose ('JACtenre'). HT, rb, Zary 2005. A magnificent rose honoring the president who declared the rose the national floral emblem of the United States. Tall, vigorous, and lightly scented. 30 petals. Zones 6 to 11. RIR=7.8
Awards: RHGM 2004

'Royal Highness'. HT, lp, Swim, 1962. Graceful blooms seem like porcelain against dark, glossy foliage. Color and size improve in moderate climates. 40 to 45 petals. Zones 5 to 10. RIR=7.7
Awards: AARS 1963, PGM 1960

Secret ('HILaroma'). HT, pb, Tracy, 1994. Well-formed, spicy-sweet blooms on strong stems; color best in cool climates: PSW, PNW, and ANE. Mahogany new foliage, easy to grow, more shade tolerant than most hybrid teas. 30 to 35 petals. Zones 6 to 10. RIR=7.9
Awards: AARS 1994, ARS/GFA, PBR, RHGM 2002

Sheer Bliss ('JACtro'). HT, w, Warriner, 1985. Tall bush with stiff glossy green foliage that mildews if unprotected. Blooms can suffer in rain; best in dry sunny climates in PSW and ASE. 35 petals. Zones 6 to 10. RIR=7.8
Awards: AARS 1987

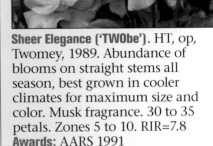

Sheer Elegance ('TWObe'). HT, op, Twomey, 1989. Abundance of blooms on straight stems all season, best grown in cooler climates for maximum size and color. Musk fragrance. 30 to 35 petals. Zones 5 to 10. RIR=7.8
Awards: AARS 1991

Sheer Magic ('JACeleco'). HT, pb, Zary, 2007. "Enchanting" is the word to describe this rose and its magnificent form, long-lasting quality, and lovely color that will enchant any visitor to your garden. Great cut flower. 30 to 35 petals. Zones 6 to 11.

Signature ('JACnor'). HT, dp, Warriner, 1996. Blooms with light and fruity fragrance appear singly on strong, straight stems. Dark green foliage on compact bush; lower foliage tends to drop after the first bloom. 30 to 35 petals. Zones 5 to 10. RIR=7.6

Spellbound ('JACpribe'). HT, pb, Zary, 2006. Blooms are exceptionally large, endowed with nonfading rich color and a nice spicy fragrance. The bush itself is vigorous, an abundant bloomer, and disease resistant. 30 to 35 petals. Zones 6 to 11.

Stainless Steel ('WEKblusi'). HT, m, Carruth, 1991. Elegantly formed blossoms with mysterious colors, best in cool climates. Tall, upright bush; has foliage that can mildew unless protected. 25 to 30 petals. Zones 6 to 10. RIR=7.5

St. Patrick ('WEKamanda'). HT, yb, Strickland, 1996. Moderately hardy, novel flower form surrounded by chartreuse foliage; heat brings out flower color. Vigorous, disease resistant. Performs best in fall where summers are hot, especially SC and ASE. 30 to 35 petals. Zones 6 to 10. RIR=8.0
Awards: AARS 1996

Strike It Rich ('WEKbepmey'). Gr, yb, Carruth, 2007. Clustered flowers with eyecatching colors that can be the focal point in any garden. Plentiful blooms with strong, spicy fragrance all season long. Tall, vigorous, and disease free. About 30 petals. Zones 6 to 10.
Awards: AARS 2007

'Suffolk'. HT, w, Perry, 1983. Large, multipetaled, high-centered form with outstanding color, this will surely be a standout in any garden. Good vigor and bloom production. 40+ petals. Zones 6 to 10. RIR=8.2

Sundance ('JACzeman'). Gr, yb, Zary, 2005. Pointed ovoid buds open to large, colorful blooms that will brighten your garden. Long lasting both outdoors or cut for a bouquet indoors. Heat tolerant. 25 petals. Zones 6 to 11.

Sunset Celebration ('FRYxotic'). HT, ab, Fryer, 1994. Covered with fragrant blooms ranging from cool to warm tones; colors are deeper in cool conditions such as the ANE. Easy to grow and disease resistant. 35 to 40 petals. Zones 6 to 10. RIR=7.8
Awards: AARS 1998

Tahitian Sunset ('JACgodde'). HT, ab, Zary, 2006. All the colors of a lovely summer sunset are captured in each bloom, and the strong fruit and rose fragrance will entice you as you get closer. A gem in any garden. 30 to 35 petal. Zones 6 to 10.
Awards: AARS 2006, RHGM 2005

Timeless ('JACecond'). HT, dp, Zary, 1997. Blooms take a long time to open fully but are worth the wait. Medium-size, compact plants are disease resistant. Prefers milder temperatures of NC and ANE. 25 petals. Zones 6 to 11 RIR=7.8
Awards: AARS 1997

Touch of Class ('KRIcarlo'). HT, op, Kriloff, 1984. Keeps its form for weeks. Weatherproof blooms; color fades in hot sunny climates of PSW and SC. Foliage mildews if unprotected. 30 petals. Zones 6 to 11. RIR=8.9
Awards: AARS 1986, PGM 1988

Tournament of Roses ('JACient'). Gr, mp, Warriner, 1988. Large sprays cover the bush; color improves with some warmth. Disease resistant. 25 to 30 petals. Zones 5 to 10. RIR=8.2
Awards: AARS 1989

Tropicana ('TANorstar'). HT, or, Tantau, 1960. The luminous blooms of this historic hybrid tea demand attention. Sweet, fruity fragrance. Performs best east of the Rockies. 30 to 35 petals. Zones 6 to 10. RIR=7.6
Awards: AARS 1963, PGM 1961

'Uncle Joe'. HT, dr, Kern, 1972. Large blooms on strong, straight stems; good color; perfect flower form in warm, humid climates. Blooms fail to open fully in dry warm climates like PSW. 50+ petals. Zones 6 to 10. RIR=7.9

Valencia ('KOReklia'). HT, ab, Kordes, 1989. Huge blooms seem as big as plates, long lasting on the bush or indoors. Strong rose fragrance. Large leaves are disease free. 35 to 40 petals. Zones 6 to 10. RIR=7.9

Veteran's Honor ('JACopper'). HT, dr, Zary, 2000. Top exhibition rose across the country in its color class, but even home gardeners love it for its magnificent color, long-lasting blossoms, and plant vigor. Raspberry fragrance. 30 to 35 petals. Zones 5 to 10. RIR=8.1

Voluptuous! ('JACtourn'). HT, pb, Zary, 2005. Multipetaled rose with exceptional form and gorgeous color that every gardener will adore. Tall, upright, full branched and disease resistant. 30 to 35 petals. Zones 6 to 10.

Whisper ('DICwisp'). HT, w, Dickson, 2002. A new, dependable variety that rose lovers are beginning to notice. Softly hued bloom with good form and substance and a hint of musk. Disease resistant. 30 to 35 petals. Zones 5 to 10. RIR=7.5
Awards: AARS 2003

Wild Blue Yonder ('WEKisosblip'). GR, m, Carruth, 2006. Informal bloom form, lovely color, ability to bloom freely, and a strong citrus and rose fragrance. 25 to 30 petals. Zones 6 to 10.
Awards: AARS 2006

World War II Memorial Rose ('WEZgrey'). HT, m, Weeks, 2000. Delicate color combination of soft white suffused with gray and a hint of lavender, sweetly fragrant. Very disease resistant. 26 to 30 petals. Zones 6 to 10.

FLORIBUNDAS AND POLYANTHAS

Second only to the hybrid tea in popularity, floribundas flower in large clusters, with smaller individual blossoms (2 to 3 inches in diameter) than those of the hybrid tea. The plants are usually 3 to 4 feet tall and work best when used at the front of a bed or border—or as a hedge. This class is unrivaled for providing massive, frequent, long-lasting, colorful garden displays. Floribundas as a class are somewhat hardier, easier to care for, and more reliable in wet weather than their hybrid tea cousins. Recent AARS winners include Julia Child, Hot Cocoa, Eureka, Honey Perfume, Marmalade Skies, and Rainbow Sorbet. A popular variety is 'Playboy', a slightly fragrant scarlet-and-gold variety hybridized by Cocker of Aberdeen, Scotland, in 1975. Two new seedlings from 'Playboy' have appeared, Playgirl and Playfair are single-petaled variations on the same theme but with dramatic color blends.

Polyanthas are bushy 2-foot plants that were developed in the late 19th century. With their narrow, finely textured leaves and clusters of 1-inch blossoms, they are sturdy, trouble-free plants for massing, edgings, and hedges.

Amber Queen ('HARroony'). F, ab, Harkness, 1983. Glossy disease-resistant foliage. Color is lighter in cooler climates and darker with warm and humid nights. Spicy-sweet fragrance. Low- to medium-size bush, 2 to 3 feet tall. 40 petals. Zones 5 to 10. RIR=7.1
Awards: AARS 1988

'Angel Face'. F, m, Swim & Weeks, 1968. Blooms have a ruffled edge and strong citrus fragrance. Plants take two seasons to establish before producing massive displays of sprays. Bush is low and rounded, 4 feet tall. A climbing counterpart is available. 25 to 30 petals. Zones 5 to 10. RIR=7.7
Awards: AARS 1969, ARS/GFM 2001

'Apricot Nectar'. F, ab, Boerner, 1965. Large fragrant blossoms. Glossy dark green, disease-resistant foliage, 3 to 4 feet tall. 30 to 40 petals. Zones 5 to 11. RIR=8.0.
Awards: AARS 1965

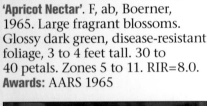

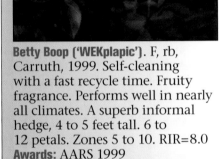

Betty Boop ('WEKplapic'). F, rb, Carruth, 1999. Self-cleaning with a fast recycle time. Fruity fragrance. Performs well in nearly all climates. A superb informal hedge, 4 to 5 feet tall. 6 to 12 petals. Zones 5 to 10. RIR=8.0
Awards: AARS 1999

Bill Warriner ('JACsur'). F, mp, Warriner and Zary, 1997. Popular since its introduction because of magnificent color, high-centered form, and ability to bloom freely. Clean and easy to maintain. 26 to 40 petals. Zones 5 to 10. RIR=7.8

Black Cherry ('JACreflo'). F, dr, Zary, 2006. Dark crimson buds with black tips open to sumptuous cherry red blooms. The velvety petals are edged with dark shades, giving added depth to the high-centered, 3½-inch blossoms. 20 to 25 petals. Zones 5 to 10.

Brass Band ('JACcofl'). F, ab, Christensen, 1994. Well-formed blooms in small clusters. Cool weather improves size and color. Fruity fragrance. 30 to 35 petals. Zones 5 to 10. RIR=7.9
Awards: AARS 1995

Brilliant Pink Iceberg ('PRObril'). F, pb, Weatherly, 1999. This is a color mutation of Iceberg. Same great landscape value, same free-flowering habit, same form and showy clusters. 17 to 25 petals. Zones 5 to 11. RIR=7.4

Blueberry Hill ('WEKcryplag'). F, m, Carruth, 1997. Upright on strong, straight stems, 4 to 5 feet tall. Good resistance to mildew. Fragrance resembles apple tart. 12 to 15 petals. Zones 5 to 10. RIR=7.8

Burgundy Iceberg ('PROse'). F, dr, Weatherly, 2006. Sport of Brilliant Pink Iceberg, with all the same attributes except color. Perfect if you are looking for this particular color. 20 to 25 petals. Zones 5 to 10.

Bolero ('MEIdeweis'). F, w, Meilland, 2004. Short in stature (1½ to 2 feet tall) but what a performer! Ideal for the front of a rose bed, it is a constant bloomer with a strong traditional rose fragrance. 100+ petals. Zones 5 to 10.

Chihuly ('WEKscemala'). F, rb, Carruth, 2004. An array of dazzling colors will greet you and everyone who sees it once this variety starts to bloom in your garden. It's like a great piece of art, echoing the works of the artist for whom this rose was named. 25 to 30 petals. Zones 5 to 10. RIR=7.7

Cinnamon Twist ('JACoutra'). F, ob, Zary, 2006. Compact plant produces single and clustered blooms with captivating colors. An excellent landscape rose that will enhance the beauty of your garden all season long. 25 to 30 petals. Zones 5 to 10.

City of San Francisco ('WEKsanpoly'). F, mr, Carruth, 2000. Large clusters of blooms dominate this round, compact bush throughout the blooming season. It is clean, vigorous, and easy to maintain. 15 to 20 petals. Zones 5 to 11.
Awards: RHGR

Class Act ('JACare'). F, w, Warriner, 1989. Fruity-scented, weatherproof blooms in small clusters. Upright, compact bush 4 to 5 feet tall. 15 to 20 petals. Zones 5 to 10. RIR=7.8
Awards: AARS 1989, PBR

Day Breaker ('FRYcentury'). F, ab, Fryer, 2004. Blooms come singly and in small clusters with a nice blending of colors. Vigorous, productive plant with attractive, glossy foliage. 30 to 35 petals. Zones 5 to 10.
Awards: AARS 2005, PBR, RHGM 2002

Ebb Tide ('WEKsmopur'). F, m, Carruth, 2006. A bloom that can only be described as mysterious, it surely will attract a lot of attention in your garden. Add to that the strong spicy fragrance and you have a real winner! More than 35 petals. Zones 5 to 11.

Eureka ('KORsuflabe'). F, ab, Kordes, 2002. Huge clusters of blooms with old-fashioned form are produced in abundance all season. The low plant is clean and easy to grow, and a wonderful landscape variety planted either alone or in masses. Over 30 petals. Zones 5 to 10. RIR=7.6
Awards: AARS 2003

'Europeana'. F, dr, de Ruiter, 1968. Produces massive sprays of red blossoms all season long. Glossy, disease-resistant foliage. Prefers heat. 25 to 30 petals. Zones 5 to 10. RIR=8.6
Awards: AARS 1968, PGM 1970

Fabulous! ('JACrex'). F, w, Zary, 2000. Robust and outrageously prolific, this easy-to-grow plant gives dozens of pristine white flowers. 25 to 30 petals. Zones 5 to 10. RIR=7.7

First Edition ('DELtep'). F, op, Delbard, 1976. Small clusters of delicate blossoms with light tea fragrance. Compact medium-size bush, 4 to 5 feet tall, has glossy dark green foliage. 28 to 30 petals. Zones 5 to 10. RIR=8.2
Awards: AARS 1977

First Kiss ('JACling'). F, pb, Warriner, 1991. Compact clusters of delicate blossoms on strong stems. Medium green foliage on compact bush, 3 to 4 feet tall. Best in cooler climates, PNW and ANE. 5 to 25 petals. Zones 5 to 10. RIR=8.2

Fragrant Wave ('JACzeeze'). F, w, Zary, 2005. Large clusters of snowy flowers with very pleasing spiced tea scent and a nice high centered form. Upright, well branched, shiny dark green foliage. 20 petals. Zones 5 to 11.
Awards: RHGM 2005

French Lace ('JAClace'). F, w, Warriner, 1980. Small clusters of delicate, well-formed hybrid-tea-size blooms. Best color and performance in cooler climates (PSW, NC, and ASE.). Protect over winter. 30 to 35 petals. Zones 5 to 10. RIR=8.1
Awards: AARS 1982, PGM 1984

'Gene Boerner'. F, mp, Boerner, 1969. Tall, upright bushes with perfect blooms in large clusters. Deepest colors in spring and fall. Spicy fragrance. 35 to 40 petals. Zones 5 to 10. RIR=8.3
Awards: AARS

George Burns ('WEKcalroc'). F, yb, Carruth, 1997. Colorful blooms come in small clusters on a medium to low upright plant. Vigorous and free flowering, it has large, deep green glossy foliage that perfectly complements the blossoms. 26 to 40 petals. Zones 5 to 10. RIR=7.7

H. C. Anderson ('POUlander'). F, dr, Poulsen, 1985. Large semidouble cupped flowers borne in huge clusters of up to 25 florets. Tall and vigorous, with dark green, glossy foliage. 12 to 18 petals. Zones 4 to 10. RIR=8.0

Honey Perfume ('JACarque'). F, ab, Zary, 2004. Pointed ovoid buds open to 3½-inch blossoms with occasional show form. Well branched, prolific, and excellent disease resistance. 25 to 30 petals. Zones 5 to 10.
Awards: AARS 2004

Hot Cocoa ('WEKpaltlez'). F, r, Carruth, 2003. Unusual color that will surprise your garden visitors. With blossoms that are produced singly and in clusters, the plant is tall, vigorous, and disease free. 25 to 30 petals. Zones 5 to 10. RIR=7.9
Awards: AARS 2003, RHGM 2004

'Iceberg'. F, w, Kordes, 1958. One of the most beloved roses of the 20th century. Profuse bloomer. Masses of large trusses constantly cover the bush. Disease resistant and cold hardy. Also available in a climbing counterpart. 20 to 25 petals. Zones 4 to 10. RIR=8.7
Awards: WFRS/HOF 1983

Intrigue ('JACum'). F, m, Warriner, 1982. Still popular after almost a quarter of a century, gardeners love it for its unique color and ability to bloom profusely. 20 petals. Zones 5 to 10. RIR=7.1
Awards: AARS 1984

'Ivory Fashion'. F, w, Boerner, 1958. Large well-formed blooms borne in clusters have some slight spicy fragrance. Vigorous, upright growth and leathery foliage. 17 petals. Zones 5 to 10. RIR=8.3
Awards: AARS 1959

Julia Child ('WEKvossutono'). F, my, Carruth, 2006. An exceptional rose chosen by the honoree. Informal form with nonfading color and a strong licorice and spice fragrance. A great new addition to any garden. 35+ petals. Zones 5 to 10.
Awards: AARS 2006

Lavaglut ('KORlech'). F, dr, Kordes, 1978. Large flowers in massive clusters on strong stems. Contrasting yellow stamens. Disease resistant and cold hardy, but prefers PNW and NC. 24 petals. Zones 4 to 11. RIR=8.7

'Little Darling'. F, yb, Duerhsen, 1956. Perfectly formed blossoms are produced in clusters of 10 to 20. Color deepens in cool weather. Plant can grow 3 to 4 feet tall and wide in warm climates. Hardy; survives Great Lakes winters. 25 to 30 petals. Zones 4 to 10. RIR=8.2
Awards: PGM 1958

Livin' Easy ('HARwelcome'). F, ob, Harkness, 1992. Neon colors. Fruity fragrance. Vigorous, disease resistant, easy to grow. Does well in a wide range of climates. 25 to 30 petals. Zones 5 to 10. RIR=8.1
Awards: AARS 1996, PBR

Margaret Merrill ('HARkuly'). F, w, Harkness, 1978. Perfectly shaped, weatherproof blooms with rich citrus and spice fragrance. Vigorous, disease resistant. Tough, deep-green foliage. 15 to 20 petals. Zones 5 to 10. RIR=8.2

Marmalade Skies ('MEImonblan'). F, ob, Meilland, 2001. Abundant blooms in big clusters throughout the season. Vigorous and easy to grow with clean, medium-green foliage. 20 to 25 petals. Zones 5 to 10. RIR=7.8
Awards: AARS 2001

Moondance ('JACtanic'). F, w, Zary, 2007. Large clusters of luminous creamy blooms scented with a hint of raspberries. Strong disease resistant plant makes an ideal landscape variety. 25 to 30 petals. Zones 5 to 10.
Awards: AARS 2007

Nicole ('KOTicole'). F, rb, Kordes, 1985. 5 to 7 feet tall with elegant clusters. Strong, thorny stems. Tough, leathery, dark foliage. Disease resistant. Grows well in all climates. 20 to 25 petals. Zones 5 to 10. RIR=8.9
Awards: PBR

Passionate Kisses ('MEIzebul'). F, pb, Meilland, 1998. One of the best in its class in recent years. Outstanding blooms produced in large clusters; long lasting and nonfading on an attractively shaped clean plant. 30 to 35 petals. Zones 5 to 10. RIR=8.2

Perfume Perfection ('JACshok'). F, m, Zary, 2000. English-style blooms abound on this medium-growing, rounded bush. Flowers with an exceptional fruity fragrance are borne in large clusters. 40+ petals. Zones 5 to 10. RIR=7.4

'Playboy'. F, rb, Cocker, 1976. Bountiful sprays of 5 to 9 blooms with an apple fragrance. Glossy dark green foliage on upright, tall (6 foot) plant. Does well in all climates. 7 to 10 petals. Zones 4 to 11. RIR=8.5
Awards: PGM 1990

Playgirl ('MORplag'). F, mp, Moore, 1986. Offspring of 'Playboy'. Contrasting golden stamens, strong fragrance. Glossy foliage. Vigorous in most climates. 5 to 7 petals. Zones 5 to 10. RIR=8.4

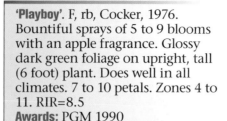

Pleasure ('JACpif'). F, mp, Warriner, 1990. Small clusters of lightly fragrant blossoms. Best color in cooler climates. Slow to establish. 30 to 35 petals. Zones 5 to 10. RIR=8.0
Awards: AARS 1990

Preference ('MEIbionel'). F, dr, Meilland, 2005. Free-flowering and self-cleaning throughout the season. Compact growth habit. Heat tolerant. Ideal for containers and small gardens. Easy to maintain and above-average disease resistance. 20 to 25 petals. Zones 5 to 10.
Awards: RHGR 2005

Pretty Lady ('SCRivo'). F, lp, Scrivens, 1997. Delicate pastel blooms borne singly and in small clusters on a medium-size rounded bush with excellent resistance to disease. About 25 petals. Zones 4 to 10.

Purple Tiger ('JACpurr'). F, m, Christensen, 1991. Large blooms in small clusters. Strong fragrance. Nearly thornless stems. Vigorous, 3 to 4 feet tall. 20 to 25 petals. Zones 5 to 10. RIR=6.9

Rainbow Sorbet ('MEIbaiprez'). F, pb, Lim, 2006. Stunning variety that becomes the center of attention in your garden. Bright, vivid blossoms; blooms continuously throughout the season. Disease resistant and cold hardy. 12 to 16 petals. Zones 5 to 10.
Awards: AARS 2006

Regensberg ('MACyoumis'). F, pb, McGredy, 1979. Compact, loaded with blossoms throughout summer. Blooms larger in cooler climates. Sweet apple fragrance. Disease resistant. 30 to 35 petals. Zones 5 to 10. RIR=7.9

Rhapsody in Blue ('FRAntasia'). F, m, Cowlishaw, 2006. A much-anticipated variety due to its breakthrough color. 2 1/2-inch blooms with a strong spicy fragrance are borne in clusters. Tall, upright plant. Cold hardy; prefers cooler weather. 15 to 20 petals. Zones 4 to 9.

Scentimental ('WEKplapep'). F, rb, Carruth, 1997. Medium-size sprays of 5 to 11 blooms, no two alike. Spicy fragrance. Protect from black spot. Prefers NC and PNW. 25 to 30 petals. Zones 4 to 11. RIR=7.7
Awards: AARS 1997

September Mourn ('MEIwhiflo'). F, w, Meilland, 2003. Low, bushy grower bears high-centered blooms singly and in small clusters. Quick to repeat, vigorous, and clean. 30 to 35 petals. Zones 5 to 10.

Sexy Rexy ('MACrexy'). F, mp, McGredy, 1984. High candelabras of 40+ blooms on strong, straight stems. Cold hardy; survives most climates. 30 to 40 petals. Zones 4 to 10. RIR=8.7
Awards: PBR 1990

Sheila's Perfume ('HARsherry'). F, yb, Sheridan, 1985. Wonderful flowers and fruit. The fragrant blooms are hybrid tea size. Vigorous, compact plant with glossy, dark green foliage. 25 petals. Zones 5 to 10. RIR=8.2
Awards: ARS/GFM 2005

Showbiz ('TANweieke'). F, mr, Tantau, 1985. Outstanding bright color on large trusses of blooms. Takes a season to establish. Disease resistant. 20 to 25 petals. Zones 5 to 10. RIR=8.3
Awards: AARS 1985

Singin' in the Rain ('MACivy'). F, ab, McGredy, 1995. Interesting color combinations vary with climate—from brown and cinnamon pink to apricot-gold and russet-orange. Blooms are weatherproof. Musk fragrance. 25 to 30 petals. Zones 5 to 10. RIR=7.7
Awards: AARS 1995

Sixteen Candles ('HARgrace'). F, lp, Harkness, 2006. Compact, upright and well branched, this prolific plant produces candelabras of flowers with a strong, sweet scent. 25 petals. Zones 5 to 10.

Summer Fashion ('JACale'). F, yb, Warriner, 1986. Fruity-scented blooms radiate color. A little heat intensifies the color. 35 to 40 petals. Zones 5 to 10. RIR=7.8

Shocking Blue ('KORblue'). F, m, Kordes, 1985. Blooms with a strong citrus fragrance in small attractive clusters. Blooms are larger in cooler climates, ANE and NC. 25 to 30 petals. Zones 6 to 10. RIR=7.4

Sun Flare ('JACjem'). F, my, Warriner, 1983. Often appears in top 10 lists. Mounded bush is covered with flowers bearing a light licorice fragrance. Foliage is polished green and disease resistant. 25 to 30 petals. Zones 5 to 10. RIR=7.8
Awards: AARS 1983, PGM 1985

Sunsprite ('KORresia'). F, dy, Kordes, 1977. Consistently voted one of 10 best yellow roses in the world. Deep, nonfading bloom color. Supersweet fragrance. Glossy green foliage. Disease resistant. Cold hardy; prefers cooler climates (PNW and NC). 25 to 30 petals. Zones 5 to 10. RIR=7.8
Awards: ARS/GFM, PGM 1979

'Sweet Vivien'. F, pb, Raffel, 1961. Small clusters of delicately colored blooms on long stems suitable for cutting. Dark green, disease-resistant foliage. Best in moderate climates. 12 to 15 petals. Zones 5 to 10. RIR=8.2

'The Fairy'. Pol, lp, Bentall, 1932. Few roses bloom as prolifically and continuously as this long-time favorite. Best of all, it's hardy and very resistant to disease. Excellent in beds and as a hedge. Grows 2 to 4 feet high and wide. 25 petals. Zones 4 to 9. RIR=8.7

Top Notch ('MACamster'). F, ob, McGredy, 2003. Medium-size blooms, fully double with good form. Excellent for cutting. Tall plant, good vigor, with dark green glossy foliage that is clean. 30 to 40 petals. Zones 5 to 10. RIR=7.3

Topsy Turvy ('WEKcocbeb'). F, dr, Carruth, 2006. An eyecatcher with loads of semidouble clustered blooms covering the entire bush all season. A great landscape rose. 10 to 15 petals. Zones 5 to 10.

Trumpeter ('MACtrum' 1977). F, or, McGredy, 1977. Long-lasting blooms in huge clusters. Attractive glossy foliage, disease resistant. Great for mass planting. Likes just a little heat. 35 to 40 petals. Zones 5 to 10. RIR=8.2
Awards: PGM 1981

Tuscan Sun ('JACthain'). F, ab, Zary, 2005. Generous clusters on long, sturdy stems adorn this medium-size plant. High-centered 4-inch flowers are more like a hybrid tea than a floribunda; long lasting with a light, spicy fragrance. 25 petals. Zones 5 to 10.
Awards: RHGR 2004

Vavoom ('WEKjutono' 2007). F, ob, Carruth, 2007. Bright, intense color makes this variety stand out. Low growing with a round habit, it is a perfect plant for a small space that needs brightening. Easy to grow and clean. More than 35 petals. Zones 5 to 10.

MINIATURES AND MINIFLORAS

Miniature roses provide novelty, versatility, color range, availability, and ease of cultivation. They can be massed in beds or as a groundcover, used for edging beds, or grown in containers and rockeries. The maximum height of the average miniature rose plant is about 15 inches, although some can grow as tall as 36 inches. A few miniatures are climbers or have climbing counterparts. Climbing miniatures reach 4 to 6 feet tall, and are ideal for small spaces as well as for growing in containers with a small trellis.

Often sold in 4-inch pots ready for transplanting, miniature roses are grown on their own roots and are hardier than either hybrid teas or floribundas. Generally, miniature roses are available year-round from mail order sources.

In 1999 the American Rose Society established minifloras as a new classification of roses. They are between miniatures and floribundas in bloom size and foliage. Their flowers are one to two inches wide, on plants that grow one to three feet tall.

Flower, form, and foliage of both miniatures and minifloras are small-scale versions of hybrid teas and floribundas. Miniatures introduced recently that exhibit the classic hybrid tea form are Baby Boomer, Harm Saville, Dancing Flame, Behold, Miss Flippins, Michel Cholet, and Butter Cream. Old favorites include 'Party Girl', 'Rise 'n' Shine', Starina, Magic Carrousel, and 'Peaches 'n' Cream'. Single-petaled miniature roses such as Gizmo have been extremely popular. There is new respect for varieties that do not possess the classic hybrid tea form. Varieties that have gained the most popularity are Santa Claus and Gourmet Popcorn. For fragrance, Scentsational by Harm Saville has both form and a heavy sweet scent.

Andie MacDowell ('MICandie'). MinFl, or, Williams, 2004. Large plant with dark green foliage and 2-inch flowers borne one to a stem or in big clusters. Great for cutting. 22 to 25 petals. Zones 5-12.
Awards: ARS/AOE

Autumn Splendor ('MICautumn'). MinFl, yb, Williams, 1999. Brilliant combinations of colors that will attract a lot of attention in the garden. Tall and bushy; blooms come singly on long stems. 26 to 40 petals. Zones 6 to 12. RIR=8.1
Awards: ARS/AOE 1999

Applause ('SAVapple'). Min, ab, Saville, 2000. Diminutive flowers on an upright but compact plant that blooms profusely all season long with little or no care. Great for container. 17 to 25 petals. Zones 4 to 10. RIR=7.5
Awards: ARS/AOE 2000

Baby Bloomer, ('JACseboy'). Min, pb, Zary, 2006. Low growing compact plant but has the ability to bloom all season long. Ideal for containers, borders and walkways. Clean and easy to maintain. 12 to 15 petals. Zones 5 to 10.
Awards: ARS/AOE 2006

Baby Boomer ('BENminn'). Min, mp, Benardella, 2003. Exhibition form blooms that are long lasting and well suited for cutting. Profuse blooms borne singly and in small sprays. Good, vigorous grower. 18 to 25 petals. Zones 5 to 10. RIR=7.6
Awards: ARS/AOE 2003

'Beauty Secret'. Min, mr, Moore, 1965. Classic variety still grown worldwide. A dependable plant bearing lots of flowers throughout the season with very little care. 18 to 25 petals. Zones 5 to 10. RIR=7.9
Awards: ARS/AOE 1975, ARS/HOF 2000

Bees Knees (JACkee). Min, yb, Zary, 1998. A variety that is creating quite a sensation on the exhibition scene. Well-formed blooms borne singly on long, strong stems; clean, dark green foliage. 10 to 25 petals. Zones 5 to 10. RIR=8.1

Behold ('SAVahold'). Min, my, Saville, 1997. Giant clusters of perfectly formed blossoms on long, strong stems; colorfast; vigorous. 15 to 20 petals. Zones 4 to 11. RIR=7.8

Best Friends ('BRIfriends' 2002). Min, yb, Bridges, 2002. Low-growing plant with attractive and well-formed blooms. Ideal for small pots or border plantings where it can show off its colors all season. Disease resistant. 18 to 25 petals. Zones 5 to 10. RIR=7.6
Awards: ARS/AOE 2002

Butter Cream ('MARbutter'). MinFl, my, Martin, 2003. New on the exhibition scene and slowly gaining a large following. Clean and high centered, the blooms come one to a stem on a tall, vigorous bush. 25 to 32 petals. Zones 5 to 10. RIR=7.8

Caliente ('BENdiez'). Min, dr, Benardella, 2004. Prolific bloomer with great exhibition form. The plant is tall but spreading, and blooms come mostly one to a stem. Nice raspberry fragrance. 25 to 32 petals. Zones 6 to 10.
Awards: ARS/AOE 2006

Chattooga ('MICtooga'). Min, dp, Williams, 2005. Tall, wide plants. The 2-inch well-formed blossoms are borne singly on long stems. Large, attractive dark green foliage complements the blooms. 25 to 32 petals. Zones 5 to 10.
Awards: ARS/AOE 2005

Child's Play ('SAVachild'). Min, pb, Saville, 1991. Very dependable variety with lots of attractive bicolor flowers that come singly and in small clusters. Medium in height, it has lush, dark green foliage on plants that is clean and easy to maintain. 18 to 25 petals. Zones 4 to 11. RIR=8.0
Awards: ARS/AOE 1993, AARS 1993

'Cinderella'. Min, w, de Vink, 1953. Still around after more than half a century, this micromini has stood the test of time and is still grown by many. A true classic. As many as 55 petals. Zones 5 to 11. RIR=8.1
Awards: ARS/HOF 2000

Class of '73 ('TUC30reunion'). MinFl, pb, Tucker, 2005. Slowly making its way up the exhibition ladder, this variety's magnificent form and long-lasting quality are sure to take it to the top. 25 to 32 petals. Zones 5 to 10.

Cupcake ('SPIcup'). Min, mp, Spies, 1981. A popular variety for its ability to bloom almost nonstop all season long. Low growing, it is ideal for containers, borders, or small corners where constant color is needed. As many as 60 petals. Zones 5 to 10. RIR=8.0
Awards: ARS/AOE 1983, ARS/HOF 2002

Dancing Flame ('TUCflame'). Min, yb, Tucker, 2001. Recognized as one of the top exhibition roses in the country. The magnificent form and color of the bloom will get a lot of attention in the garden. Good grower, lots of vigor, clean and good repeat. 18 to 25 petals. Zones 4 to 11. RIR=7.6

Doris Morgan ('BRImorgan'). Min, dp, Bridges, 2003. Fabulous color on a well-formed exhibition bloom. The bush is upright as well as spreading. Lots of dark green, shiny foliage that sets up the blossoms beautifully. 20 to 28 petals. Zones 5 to 10. RIR=7.8

Double Gold ('SAVadouble'). MinFl, yb, White, 2003. Magnificent high-centered blooms with a superb blending of colors. The 2-inch flowers have a nice fragrance. The bush is covered with lush, dark green shiny foliage that looks healthy and clean. 25 to 32 petals. Zones 6 to 11. RIR=7.4

Dr. John Dickman ('BRIman'). MinFl, m, Bridges, 2002. Long, tapered buds open to high-centered lavender blooms with darker shadings on the petal edges. The plant is tall with large dark green foliage that is sometimes susceptible to mildew. 20 to 25 petals. Zones 5 to 10.

Fairhope ('TALfairhope'). Min, ly, Taylor, 1989. A top exhibition rose in the U.S., this variety has clean, creamy blooms that turn white during hot weather. Impeccable form. 16 to 28 petals. Zones 5 to 11. RIR=8.2

Gizmo ('WEKcatlart') Min, ob, Carruth, 1998. Low growing but vigorous bush that produces an abundance of small single petal blooms all season long. Great landscape rose! 5 petals. Zones 4 to 11. RIR=7.9.
Awards: RHGR

Glowing Amber ('MANglow'). Min, rb, Mander, 1997. Perfectly formed blooms and vivid color combinations on long, delicate stems. Prolific. 25 to 30 petals. Zones 5 to 10. RIR=8.0

Gourmet Popcorn ('WEOpop'). Min, w, Desamero, 1986. Masses of sprays (30 to 60 blooms) cover a vigorous bush with shiny dark green foliage. Disease resistant, cold hardy. 12 to 20 petals. Zones 4 to 10. RIR=8.7

Harm Saville ('WEKclauni'). MinFl, dr, Bedard and Carruth, 2005. A variety that will please any home gardener for its ability to bloom profusely. Vigorous, easy to grow and maintain. 18 to 25 petals. Zones 5 to 10.
Awards: ARS/AOE 2005

Hilde ('BENhile'). Min, rb, Benardella, 2001. Slow to start but rewards you with magnificent high-centered blooms once it's established. Cooler weather brings some darker shadings on the outer petals. 18 to 24 petals. Zones 6 to 11. RIR=7.6

Hot Tamale ('JACpoy'). Min, yb, Zary, 1994. Produces single blooms in warm climates, small sprays where cooler. Vigorous spreader to 3 feet tall. 25 petals. Zones 5 to 10. RIR=8.3
Awards: ARS/AOE 1994

'Iced Raspberry' (SAVaras). Min, pb, White, 2006. Eyecatching color combination on a low-growing but spreading plant. Excellent form that holds well, ideal for corsages and boutonnieres. 18 to 25 petals. Zones 6 to 11.
Awards: ARS/AOE 2006

Irresistible ('TINresist'). Min, w, Bennett, 1989. Vigorous; 3 feet tall. Perfect, long-lasting blooms grow in candelabras. 45 to 50 petals. Zones 5 to 10. RIR=9.0

Jean Kenneally ('TINeally'). Min, ab, Bennett, 1986. Tall, elegant sprays of exquisite apricot blossoms. Thrives in just about all climates. Blooms are close to perfection. 25 petals. Zones 5 to 10. RIR=9.1
Awards: ARS/AOE 1986, ARS/HOF 2005

'Jeanne Lajoie'. ClMin, mp, Sima, 1975. Abundant blooms if canes are trained horizontally. Vigorous, cold hardy. Grows 8 to 10 feet tall. 40 petals. Zones 4 to 11. RIR=9.1
Awards: ARS/AOE 1977, ARS/HOF 2001

Jilly Jewel ('BENmfig'). Min, pb, Benardella, 1996. Abundant blooms, singly and in clusters, with good form and mouthwatering color all season long. Tall and vigorous, it also tends to spread, so give it plenty of room. Susceptible to rust. 18 to 27 petals. Zones 5 to 10. RIR=7.8

Kristin ('BENmagic'). Min, rb, Benardella, 1993. Great color combination intensifies in hot climates. In cooler climates blooms tend not to open fully. Vigorous, disease-resistant plant. 27 to 30 petals. Zones 5 to 10. RIR=7.9
Awards: ARS/AOE 1993

Lemon Gems ('JACmiryl'). Min, my, Walden, 2000. Excellent garden variety with great ability to bloom profusely. Color holds well even in the dead of summer. Low growing and spreading. Use in front of a rose bed or in a container or even a hanging basket. 26 to 40 petals. Zones 5 to 11.
Awards: ARS/AOE 2000

Liberty Bell ('BENpete' 2002, miniflora). MinFl, rb, Benardella, 2002. Big tapered buds open to multipetaled deep dark-red flowers that sometimes verge on black. Tall and vigorous, blooms comes singly on long stems with large, dark green foliage that can attract mildew. 20 to 28 petals. Zones 4 to 11. RIR=7.4

Life Lines ('SPRolife'). ClMin, or, Sproul, 2005. Striped flowers comes in large clusters and are semidouble. The plant grows to 10 feet tall, and blooms along mature canes easily clothe the whole bush. Excellent against a wall, or on a trellis or pergola. 12 to 15 petals. Zones 5 to 10.
Awards: ARS/AOE 2005

Little Jackie ('SAVor' 1982). Min, ob, Saville, 1982. Upright bush with exhibition-form blooms and eyecatching color. Good vigor and repeat, though the plant is susceptible to mildew. 20 petals. Zones 5 to 10. RIR=7.9
Awards: ARS/AOE 1984, ARS/HOF 2003

Luis Desamero ('TINluis'). Min, ly, Bennett, 1989. Perfect classic blooms grow naturally one to a stem. Plants are nice and tall, upright, healthy, and vigorous. Abundant foliage. 28 petals. Zones 5 to 10. RIR=7.9

Magic Carrousel ('MORrousel'). Min, rb, Moore, 1975. Striking color. Beautiful display when fully open. Vigorous and hardy. 25 petals. Zones 5 to 10. RIR=8.5
Awards: ARS/AOE 1975, ARS/HOF 1999

Memphis Music ('WELmusic'). MinFl, rb, Wells, 2007. Unique combinations of colors on a strong, healthy-looking bush. Large blooms with complementary dark green foliage. Watch for mildew. 22 to 30 petals. Zones 4 to 11.

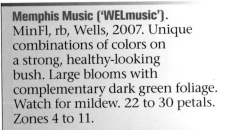

Merlot ('BENfebu'). Min, dr, Benardella, 2002. Bright red blooms with white reverse borne singly and in small clusters on an upright plant with lush dark green foliage that is disease resistant. Vigorous, prolific and easy to grow. 18 to 25 petals. Zones 4 to 10. RIR=7.5
Awards: ARS/AOE 2002

Michel Cholet ('FOUmich'). Min, ab, Jacobs, 2001. Gorgeous color on a well-formed flower, borne singly on an upright though spreading plant. Vigorous, good repeat, clean. 18 to 25 petals. Zones 5 to 11. RIR=7.5
Awards: ARS/AOE 2001

Minnie Pearl ('SAVahowdy'). Min, pb, Saville, 1982. Blooms singly or in large clusters. Glossy foliage; flower form holds even in heat. Vigorous, cold hardy. 25 to 30 petals. Zones 4 to 10. RIR=9.0
Awards: ARS/HOF 2004

Memphis King ('WELking'). MinFl, dr, Wells, 2003. Exhibition-type blooms on a vigorous bush with large dark green foliage that can attract mildew. 22 to 30 petals. Zones 4 to 11. RIR=7.7

Miss Flippins ('TUCkflip'). Min, mr, Tucker, 1997. Blooms hold classic form for days. Foliage is large but balanced with bloom size. Vigorous grower, 2 to 3 feet tall and wide. 20 petals. Zones 5 to 10. RIR=8.1

Moonlight Scentsation ('SAVamoon'). MinFl, w, White, 2004. Bloom form is mostly decorative, but the big attraction here is its overwhelming fragrance. Tall and upright, the plants have some vigor but can suffer severe dieback in winter. 18 to 28 petals. Zone 5 to 10.

'Party Girl'. Min, yb, Saville, 1982. Immaculate flower form on large candelabras with as many as 20 florets at once. Best in cooler climates. Not cold hardy. 23 petals. Zones 6 to 10. RIR=8.2
Awards: ARS/AOE 1981, ARS/HOF 2000

'Peaches 'n' Cream'. Min, pb, Woolcock, 1977. Tapered buds open to full blossoms. In cold, damp climates florets will not open fully. Vigorous and compact. 50+ petals. Zones 5 to 10. RIR=7.9
Awards: ARS/AOE 1977

Picotee ('BENpico'). Min, rb, Benardella, 2004. Attractive bicolor blooms with some good exhibition form. For garden display, it's unbeatable because of its ability to bloom profusely. Excellent specimen for borders and containers. 18 to 22 petals. Zones 5 to 11.
Awards: ARS/AOE 2004

Rainbow's End ('SAValife'). Min, yb, Saville, 1986. Upright bush with blooms on short stems. Ideal for containers. Climbing counterpart recently available. 35 petals. Zones 5 to 10. RIR=8.7
Awards: ARS/AOE 1986, ARS/HOF 2005

Ralph Moore ('SAVaralph'). Min, mr, Saville, 2000. Low growing plant, well branched and loaded with small red blooms that come singly and in clusters. The dark green shiny foliage is disease resistant and sets off the bloom beautifully. 20 to 25 petals. Zones 4 to 10. RIR= 7.6
Awards: ARS/AOE 2000

Red Casade ('MOORcap'). ClMin, dr, Moore, 1976. Vigorous variety that can spread to 5 feet across, a mound of color all season. Excellent as a small climber and for hedges, hanging baskets, and groundcover. Easy to grow. 40 petals. Zones 4 to 11. RIR=7.6
Awards: ARS/AOE 1976, ARS/HOF 2004

'Rise 'n' Shine'. Min, my, Moore, 1978. Brilliant clear yellow blossoms and glossy dark green foliage on a medium-size bush. 35 petals. Zones 5 to 10. RIR=8.4
Awards: ARS/AOE 1978, ARS/HOF 2000

Ruby ('BENmjul'). Min, mr, Benardella, 2001. A dependable rose that continues to bloom without much attention. Vigorous, clean, and very easy to grow. 18 to 22 petals. Zones 4 to 11. RIR=7.4
Awards: ARS/AOE 2001

Santa Claus ('POUlclaus'). Min, dr, Poulsen, 1991. An all-around landscape rose producing loads of well-formed blooms singly and in clusters. Great disease resistance, easy to grow, and dependable. 15 to 25 petals. Zones 4 to 10. RIR=7.8

'Snow Bride'. Min, w, Jolly, 1983. Petals reflex to give porcelainlike qualities to marvelous blooms. Survives heat and cold. Compact, low growing. Disease resistant. 20 petals. Zones 5 to 10. RIR=8.5
Awards: ARS/AOE 1983, ARS/HOF 2003

Solar Flair ('BENbaas'). MinFl, yb, Benardella, 2005. Large well-formed blooms that are long lasting. Excellent for exhibition as well as for cutting. Extremely attractive color. 18 to 25 petals. Zones 5 to 10.

Salute ('SAVasalute'). Min, dr, White, 2004. Named for the men and women of the armed forces, it is a low-growing compact bush that blooms profusely throughout the growing season. Great for containers or the front of a rose bed where it can show off its colors all season. 18 to 25 petals. Zones 4 to 11.
Awards: ARS/AOE 2004

Scentsational ('SAVamor'). Min, m, Saville, 1998. Great flower form, substance, fragrance, and vigor, but can get a bit large in cooler climates. 2 to 3 feet tall. 30 to 35 petals. Zones 5 to 10. RIR=7.6

Starina ('MEIgabi'). Min, or, Meilland, 1965. Blooms singly or in small clusters of 3 to 5 florets. An international award-winning rose. Dwarf habit. 20 petals. Zones 5 to 10. RIR=8.3
Awards: ARS/HOF 1999

Starship ('BRIstar'). MinFl, yb, Bridges, 2002. Tall and upright, the 2½-inch-diameter blooms have substance and spectacular color. Foliage is healthy dark green and needs minimal care against diseases. 20 to 28 petals. Zones 5 to 11. RIR=7.7

Sun Sprinkles ('JAChal' 2001). Min, dy, Walden, 2001. Outstanding nonfading blooms. Clean, easy to grow and maintain. Profuse blooms make it perfect for containers, borders, and walkways. 30 to 35 petals. Zones 4 to 11. RIR=7.8
Awards: AARS 2001, ARS/AOE 2001

Sweet Diana ('SAVdiana'). Min, dy, Saville, 2002. A low-growing bush with glossy medium green foliage and bright nonfading daffodil yellow blooms makes this an ideal specimen for containers or the front of a rose bed. Vigorous and disease free. 18 to 25 petals. Zones 4 to 11. RIR=7.8
Awards: ARS/AOE 2002

This is The Day ('SPRoday'). Min, or, Sproul, 2003. Unique color with true miniature blooms on a healthy, upright bush. Blooms profusely. Excellent variety for exhibition or garden display. 18 to 24 petals. Zones 5 to 10. RIR=7.7
Awards: ARS/AOE 2003

'Tiffany Lynn'. MinFl, pb, Jolly, 1985. Large exhibition-form blooms with gorgeous color on a tall, lanky bush that is susceptible to mildew. Strictly for exhibitors. 21 petals. Zones 4 to 11. RIR= 8.1

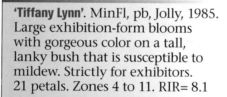

Ty ('TUCkty'). Min, dy, Tucker, 2006. Fast becoming the latest favorite among exhibitors and home gardeners, this variety boasts high-centered blooms borne singly and in clusters. Strong, vigorous, and healthy-looking plant with good repeat. 25 to 30 petals. Zones 4 to 11.

X-Rated ('TINx'). Min, pb, Bennett, 1994. Excellent flower form on large candelabras. Intense color in cooler climates. Strong fragrance. 26 to 40 petals. Zones 4 to 10. RIR=7.9

SPECIES AND OLD GARDEN ROSES

Grow some history in your garden! Species roses—as their name implies—were the first wild roses, from which all old garden roses and eventually modern roses were bred. In 1966 the American Rose Society defined old garden roses as those varieties that existed before 1867, the year of the first hybrid tea. Certain old garden roses were introduced after 1867, but if they belong to an established classification existing before 1867, they are still classified as old garden roses.

You'll find a lot of variety among old garden roses. Some bloom only once in spring; others repeat sporadically after the big spring flush, while still others bloom continually all season. Many varieties have a heavy, sweet fragrance, and quite a few (especially once-blooming types) produce attractive hips in fall. Some are cold hardy and others tender. Some are highly disease resistant, others are not. Flower form can be quartered, cupped, imbricated or expanded, reflexed, globular, or compact. And while most are large, arching shrubs, some are rounded and compact.

Types of old garden roses in this section:

Alba: Blooms once in spring. Upright habit, dense foliage, hardy, more shade-tolerant, and disease resistant. Zones 3 to 8.
Bourbon: Repeat-blooming plants, 2 to 15 feet tall, fragrant, quartered blooms. Zones 6 to 9.
Centifolia: Once-blooming, very fragrant plants 4 to 8 feet tall. Centifolia means 100 petals. Prone to mildew. Zones 4 to 9.
China: Repeat bloomers 1 to 3 feet tall, with somewhat weak stems. Clusters of blossoms, spicy fragrance. Prone to mildew. Zones 7 to 9.
Damask: Intense fragrance. 3 to 6 feet tall. Some are reblooming. Prone to mildew. Zones 6 to 9.
Gallica: Small (3 to 4 feet tall) bushy plants. Once-blooming, fragrant, brilliant colors. Prone to mildew. Zones 4 to 8.
Hybrid foetida: Tall, vigorous plants. The source of yellow color in modern roses; descendents are also highly susceptible to black spot. Zones 3 to 9.

Hybrid perpetual: Repeat bloomers, 6 feet tall. Mostly pinks and reds, fragrant. Hardiness varies.
Moss: Plants 3 to 6 feet tall, some repeat bloomers. Mossy growth on penduncle and sepals. Fragrant. Prone to mildew. Zones 4 to 8.
Noisette: Rambles up to 20 feet. Large, repeat-blooming clusters. Very fragrant. Zones 7 to 9.
Portland: Repeat-blooming plants 4 feet tall, short penduncles. Fragrant. Zones 6 to 9.
Tea: Repeat bloomers. 4 feet tall. Large fragrant blooms on weak stems. Some climb. Zones 7 to 10.

'Autumn Damask' (Quatre Saisons). Damask, mp, prior to 1600. Large florets with sometimes crumpled petals on a 4-foot-tall plant. Flowering is best in spring and late fall. Highly fragrant. 35 to 40 petals. Zones 4 to 10. RIR=8.2

'Baronne Prévost'. Hybrid perpetual, mp, Desprez, 1842. Big, flat, open flowers are quartered with a button eye. Erect, bushy, thorny 4- to 6-foot-tall plant. Recurrent bloomer. Rich damask fragrance. Protect from black spot. 100+ petals. Zones 5 to 10. RIR=8.6

'Austrian Copper' (*Rosa foetida* 'Bicolor'). Species, rb, Gerard, prior to 1596. Blooms once in the spring but the display is dazzling. Grows 6 to 8 feet tall (taller in warm climates), twice as wide. Unpleasant odor. 5 petals. Zones 4 to 11. RIR=7.8

'Apothecary's Rose' (*Rosa gallica* 'Officinalis'). Gallica, dp, prior to 1500. Also known as the Red Rose of Lancaster. Erect growth to 5 feet tall. Can spread by suckers. Blooms prolifically once in spring or early summer. Blooms semidouble, very fragrant. 35 to 40 petals. Zones 3 to 8. RIR=8.7

'Cardinal de Richelieu'. Gallica, m, Parmentier, 1840. One bloom cycle on a 4- to 5-foot plant in spring and summer, but worth the color display. Sweet fragrance. 40 to 50 petals. Zones 4 to 9. RIR=8.0

'Catherine Mermet'. Tea, lp, Guillot, 1869. Blooms spring through fall with shapely florets. Flower size can vary with climate. Coppery-tinged foliage is disease resistant. Grows 4 to 7 feet tall. Light fragrance. 25 to 30 petals. Zones 7 to 10. RIR=7.9

'Celsiana'. Damask, lp, unknown, prior to 1750. Highly scented small clusters of large open semidouble flowers. A beautiful plant in every way. About 6 feet tall. 40 to 50 petals. Zones 4 to 10. RIR=8.7

'Comte de Chambord'. Portland, pb, Moreau-Robert, 1860. Attractive quartered-flower form, heavy old rose perfume. Disease resistant. Blooms constantly. Plant is vigorous and of medium height. 40 to 50 petals. Zones 5 to 9. RIR=8.3

'Crested Moss' *(Rosa centifolia 'Christata')*. Moss, mp, Vibert, 1827. Also known as "Chapeau de Napoléon." One bloom cycle in the spring and summer. In warm climates can be grown as a small climber, 5 to 6 feet tall. Very fragrant. 35 to 40 petals. Zones 5 to 9. RIR=8.7

'Ferdinand Pichard'. Hybrid perpetual, rb, Tanne, 1921. One of the few striped old garden roses to repeat bloom. Tall (6 feet), upright plant with disease-resistant foliage. Distinct fragrance. 25 petals. Zones 4 to 9. RIR=7.6

'Gloire de Dijon'. Climbing tea, op, Jacotot, 1853. Great first flush of fragrant blooms in spring, then only a few flowers in autumn. 8 to 12 feet tall. Quartered flower form. 17 to 30 petals. Zones 4 to 10. RIR=7.8
Awards: WFRS/OGR

'Great Maiden's Blush'. Alba, w, prior to 1738. Also known as "Cuisse de Nymphe Émue." Loose flower form, surrounded by blue-gray leaves. Blooms once. Grows 6 feet tall. Strong, sweet fragrance. 35 to 40 petals. Zones 5 to 9. RIR=8.9

'Harison's Yellow'. Hybrid foetida, dy, Harison, 1830. Cold hardy plant that tends to spread out rapidly, so give it space. Grows 10 to 12 feet tall and just as wide. 20 to 35 petals. Zones 4 to 9. RIR=8.3

'La Belle Sultane'. Hybrid gallica, dr, 1795. Lovely, but a one-time-only display of semidouble florets. Contrasting yellow stamens. Tall (5 to 6 feet) and upright. 7 to 15 petals. Zones 4 to 10. RIR=8.3

'Gruss an Teplitz'. Bourbon, mr, Geschwind, 1897. Only modestly fragrant small clusters of blooms. Recurrent. Stems tend to droop. 5 to 7 feet tall. 30 to 40 petals. Zones 6 to 10. RIR=8.0
Awards: WFRS/OGR

'La Reine'. Hybrid perpetual, mp, Laffay, 1842. Silky-textured, quartered blooms in profusion in spring but somewhat less at other times of the season. 70 to 80 petals. Zones 5 to 9. RIR=8.0

'Louise Odier'. Bourbon, dp, Margottin, 1851. Fragrant blossoms resembling camellias in clusters often too heavy for the stems to support. Blooms spring into fall. 6 feet tall. 5 to 40 petals. Zones 5 to 10. RIR=8.4

'Mme Alfred Carrière'. Noisette, w, Schwartz, 1879. Climber with continuous recurrent flowering. Large florets, rather loosely formed. Strong fragrance. 10 to 12 feet tall. 35 to 40 petals. Zones 6 to 10. RIR=8.9
Awards: WFRS/OGR

'Mme Hardy'. Damask, w, Hardy, 1832. Rich green central pip with petals folded inward. Blooms once in spring. Strong scent. Grows 5 to 6 feet tall. 100 petals or more. Zones 4 to 9. RIR=8.9
Awards: WFRS/OGR

'Mme Isaac Pereire'. Bourbon, dp, Garçon, 1881. This bold, tall bush blooms spring to fall on strong stems. Strong fragrance. Can be trained as a climber 7 to 8 feet tall in warmer climates. 40 petals. Zones 6 to 10. RIR=8.4

'Mme Pierre Oger'. Bourbon, pb, Oger, 1878. Florets resemble translucent water lilies. Very fragrant. Recurrent bloomer. Vigorous, hardy, and disease resistant. 5 feet tall. 35 to 40 petals. Zones 6 to 10. RIR=8.0

'Marchesa Boccella'. Hybrid perpetual, lp, Desprez, 1842. Featherylike sepals envelop the lovely soft pink, quartered, fragrant blooms. 50+ petals. Zones 4 to 9. RIR=9.0

'Marechal Niel'. Noisette, my, Pradel, 1864. Climber. Florets in clusters, very fragrant, recurrent. Foliage is dark coppery green. Vigorous, to 15 feet tall. Prefers heat. 35 to 40 petals. Zones 5 to 11. RIR=7.8

'Mermaid'. Hybrid bracteata, ly, Paul, 1918. Large, fragrant, single-petaled blossoms appear spring to fall. Beautiful climber, 20 to 30 feet tall. Watch out for thorns. Not cold hardy. 5 petals. Zones 8 to 11. RIR=8.6

'Mutabilis'. Hybrid china, yb, prior to 1894. Large spreading bush that can climb up a house wall. Single flowers exhibit a changing color scheme with age, from yellow to orange to red. 4 to 8 petals. Zones 7 to 10. RIR=8.9

'Old Blush'. China, mp, Parsons, 1752. Thornless, recurrent bloomer to 4 feet tall. A climbing form for Zones 8 to 10 is available. 25 to 30 petals. Zones 7 to 9 with protection. RIR=8.2
Awards: WFRS/OGR

'Paul Neyron'. Hybrid perpetual, dp, Levet, 1869. Huge florets with cupped form come singly on strong, straight stems. Bloom is intermittent, lightly scented. Plants grow 6 feet tall. 50 petals. Zones 4 to 9. RIR=8.2

'Reve d'Or'. Noisette, my, Ducher, 1869. Shapely blossoms may have a tinge of pink in cooler climates. Some recurrent blooming. Very fragrant. Vigorous but tender climber, 12 feet tall. 25 to 30 petals. Zones 7 to 9. RIR=9.3

'Rosa Mundi' *(Rosa gallica versicolor)*. Species, pb, 1581. A striped rose from the distant past with stems sometimes too weak to support blooms upright. 12 to 20 petals. Zones 4 to 10. RIR=9.0

'Rose de Rescht'. Portland, dp, reintroduced 1940. Tight clusters are borne on short stems. Small, compact bush reaching only 3 feet high. 25 to 40 petals. Zones 5 to 10. RIR=8.8

'Rose du Roi'. Portland, mr, Lelier, 1815. Dwarf compact bush, 3 feet tall. Recurrent blooming, very fragrant. Prefers mild climates. 25 to 30 petals. Zones 6 to 9. RIR=7.8

'Safrano'. Tea, ab, Beauregard, 1839. Fragrant blooms fade in sunlight. Spent blooms need to be removed to promote reflowering. Small bush growing to 4 feet tall. 17 to 25 petals. Zones 7 to 11. RIR=7.0

'Salet'. Moss, mp, Lacharme, 1854. Medium-size bush, 4 to 5 feet tall, covered with small bloom clusters. Moderately recurrent. Fragrant. Can suffer from mildew. 35 to 40 petals. Zones 4 to 10. RIR=8.2

'Sombreuil'. LCl, w, Robert, 1880. A favorite climber in moderate climates (PSW, SC, and ASE). Grows 10 to 12 feet tall. Self-cleaning. 45 to 50 petals. Zones 7 to 9. RIR=8.8

'Souvenir de la Malmaison'. Bourbon, lp, Béluze, 1843. Blooms open to flat, quartered masterpieces with a spicy fragrance. Hates rain. 4 feet tall. A climbing counterpart is available. 35 to 40 petals. Zones 6 to 9. RIR=8.7
Awards: WFRS/OGR

'Stanwell Perpetual'. Hybrid spinosissima, w, Lee, 1838. Good repeat flowering characteristic, delicate fragrance, very thorny. 6 to 7 feet tall. 25 to 40 petals. Zones 4 to 10. RIR=8.6

'Tuscany Superb'. Hybrid gallica, m, Rivers, prior to 1837. Large, dark blooms with contrasting golden yellow stamens appear once in summer. 4 to 5 feet tall. 35 to 40 petals. Zones 4 to 9. RIR=8.5

'Zéphirine Drouhin'. Bourbon, mp, Bizot, 1868. Long-flowering climber, 10 to 12 feet tall. Nearly thornless stems. Distinctive fragrance in warm climates. Tolerates shade. 30 to 35 petals. Zones 5 to 10. RIR=8.1

Classic and Modern Shrubs

Shrub is a generic classification given to a heterogeneous group of roses that don't fit neatly into any other category. Some are compact, growing 3 feet tall; others sprawl to as much as 12 to 15 feet wide. What stands out about this class is its vigor, repeat cycles of large bloom clusters, disease resistance, hardiness, and low maintenance. Some shrub roses make ideal hedges; others perform well as ground covers and in beds. There are six popular subdivisions—five are sometimes referred to as "classic shrubs," and one is often called "modern shrubs."

Classic shrubs

Because many of the earliest varieties were developed early in the twentieth century, several subdivisions of shrub roses are referred to informally as classic shrubs—hybrid rugosa, hybrid kordesii, hybrid musk, hybrid moyesii, and hybrid wichurana. These subdivisions are generally vigorous, large, and disease resistant. Known for their ability to grow in the most hostile of environments—both hot and cold—they survive in spite of neglect. But with regular care they can make wonderful landscape possibilities come true. Within this group the diversity of form, color, and habit can be vast—from the simplicity of single-petaled elegance to graceful multipetaled classics reminiscent of their near cousins, the old garden roses.

The hybrid rugosa derived its name from its characteristic deep-furrowed foliage. It is both hardy and disease resistant. Hybrid kordesii plants are large, dense, and ideally suited to landscaping or training as climbers. Hybrid musks are also large, repeat-blooming varieties that can grow up to 20 feet in every direction and are commonly trained onto trellises or into trees. The hybrid wichuranas are known for their long, sprawling canes and dense, glossy, healthy green foliage. Because of their sprawling habit and disease-resistance, they are often used as ground covers as well as climbers.

Modern shrubs

As a result of the pioneering work of David Austin in England, in the early 1970s a new group of shrub roses became popular that are often referred to as modern shrubs. By crossing old garden roses with modern roses such as hybrid teas and floribundas, Austin's roses were marked by the fragrances and romantic flower forms of old garden roses, but with the recurrent blooming, vigor, hardiness, and color range of modern hybrids.

Other breeders have contributed to this modern shrub group, including the extra hardy shrubs of Dr. Griffith Buck in Iowa, ground covers from Kordes in Germany and Meilland in France, Romantica roses from Meilland, and some Moore roses from California. Like Austin's roses, these were developed by crossing old garden roses with modern ones, retaining the best features of both. Old-fashioned fragrances such as myrrh, citrus, apple, musk, and damask enhance their appeal.

Many modern shrub roses are root hardy in Zones 4 to 10, but perform best with winter protection in Zone 6 and farther north. Most are vigorous and reasonably disease resistant.

Some roses popularly regarded as shrubs are technically registered as floribundas or hybrid teas, but because they behave like and are marketed with other shrub roses, they are listed in this section.

Meidiland Landscape Roses

La Sevillana   **White Meidiland**   **Cherry Meidiland**   **Pink Meidiland**

Although some are technically classified as floribundas, the Meidiland series of landscape roses is one example of breeding in the category often referred to as "modern shrubs." Wonderfully low maintenance, pest resistant, disease tolerant, and cold hardy, they provide nonstop, long-lasting, brilliant blooms. Some, such as La Sevillana, provide a beautiful show of red hips in the fall.

Landscape opportunities range from hedges to beds and groundcovers. Shrub roses marketed as groundcover and hedge roses are usually different in habit from the traditional bush types.

Groundcovers boast a low-growing habit and spread over large areas; they often have *Rosa wichurana* in their genetic background. Hedge roses form a compact hedge if planted close together, about 12 to 18 inches apart.

White groundcovers in the Meidiland series include Alba Meidiland (RIR=8.4), Ice Meidiland, and White Meidiland (RIR=8.4); in red there are Magic Meidiland, La Sevillana and Red Meidiland (RIR=7.4). Pink hedge roses include Bonica, Royal Bonica, Coral Meidiland, Cherry Meidiland, and Pink Meidiland (RIR=8.6). All are hardy Zones 5 to 10.

Abraham Darby ('AUScot'). Shrub, op, Austin, 1985. Huge blooms are the hallmark of this multipetaled variety. Highly fragrant. Can be trained on a wall or trellis. 6 to 8 feet tall. 50 to 100 petals. Zones 5 to 11. RIR=8.0

'Ballerina'. Hybrid musk, mp, Bentall, 1937. Outstanding landscape plant. Hydrangealike clusters throughout the season. Vigorous. Disease resistant. Can be trained as a climber reaching 10 feet, or groomed as a neat 5-foot shrub. 5 to 12 petals. Zones 4 to 9. RIR=8.7

Belle Story ('AUSelle'). Shrub, lp, Austin, 1985. Yellow stamens give this bloom a very attractive appearance. Intensely fragrant. 4 to 6 feet tall. 35 petals. Zones 5 to 11. RIR=8.6

Bonica ('MEldomonac'). F, mp, Meilland, 1985. Giant clusters, some fragrance. Plant prefers to spread with long arching canes 3 to 4 feet high rather than grow tall. Ideal as a groundcover. Foliage is small and disease free. 40+ petals. Zones 4 to 9. RIR=8.4 **Awards:** WFRS/HOF 2003, AARS 1986

Alnwick Castle ('AUSgrab'). Shrub, pb, Austin, 2001. Strong scent of old rose fragrance with just a hint of raspberry. Pretty pink cupped blooms are long lasting. 6 to 7 feet tall. 41+ petals. Zones 4 to 11.

Carefree Beauty ('BUCbi'). Shrub, mp, Buck, 1977. Medium-size clusters bloom nonstop. Medium-green foliage. Disease resistant. Upright, 5 to 6 feet tall. Hardy. 9 to 15 petals. Zones 4 to 9. RIR=8.6

Charles Austin ('AUSfather'). Shrub, ab, Austin, 1981. Lightly scented flowers in small clusters fade to light pink. 4 to 6 feet tall. 70 petals. Zones 5 to 11. RIR=8.0

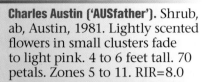

Charles Rennie Macintosh ('AUSren'). Shrub, pb, Austin, 1988. Cupped flowers with powerful fragrance. Remove spent blooms to promote next cycle. Vigorous, thorny bush. 4 to 6 feet tall. 50 petals. Zones 4 to 9. RIR=7.9

Carefree Delight ('MEIpotal'). Shrub, pb, Meilland, 1994. Flowers in small clusters cover the 3- to 4-foot mounded plants spring to fall. Vigorous, disease resistant. 5 petals. Zones 4 to 10. RIR=8.2
Awards: AARS 1996

Charles Darwin ('AUSpeet'). Shrub, my, Austin, 2001. Noted for the strong, long stems supporting massive, fragrant small clusters of blooms. 5 to 6 feet tall. 41+ petals. Zones 5 to 10. RIR=7.5

Constance Spry ('AUSfirst'). Shrub, lp, Austin, 1961. Austin's first introduction. One bloom cycle in the spring. Will sprawl 10 to 12 feet in all directions. Strong myrrh fragrance. 50 petals. Zones 4 to 9. RIR=8.5

Carefree Wonder ('MEIpitac'). Shrub, pb, Meilland, 1990. Large radiant flowers with a white eye and cream reverse are borne in small clusters. Superb disease resistance, hardiness, and neat growth habit 3 to 4 feet tall, 2 to 3 feet wide. 20 to 25 petals. Zones 3 to 9. RIR=8.0
Awards: AARS 1991

'Cornelia'. Hybrid musk, pb, Pemberton, 1925. Large fragrant flowers in flat clusters all season. Extremely vigorous, 8 to 10 feet tall in warm climates. In fall the plant provides a display of hips. 20 to 25 petals. Zones 6 to 9. RIR=8.7

DayDream ('BAleam'). Shrub, m, Lim, 2004. Massive clusters of fuchsia pink, scented blooms cover the plant all season long without maintenance. 3 to 4 feet tall. 11 petals. Zones 5 to 11. **Awards:** AARS 2005

Ellen ('AUScup'). Shrub, ab, Austin, 1984. Small clusters of very large, soft apricot blooms; heavy fragrance. 5 to 6 feet tall. 25 to 40 petals. Zones 5 to 10. RIR=7.5

Evelyn ('AUSsaucer'). Shrub, ab, Austin, 1992. Large blooms are profuse in early summer, with occasional repeat. Powerful old-rose scent. 4 to 5 feet tall, 3 feet wide. 40+ petals. Zones 5 to 10. RIR=7.9

Fair Bianca ('AUSca'). Shrub, w, Austin, 1982. Myrrh-scented, symmetrical blossoms. 4 to 5 feet tall. 50+ petals. Zones 4 to 10. RIR=7.8

Fisherman's Friend ('AUSchild'). Shrub, dr, Austin, 1987. Deep crimson cupped blooms with heavy damask fragrance. 4 to 5 feet tall. 50+ petals. Zones 5 to 10. RIR=7.8

Flower Carpet ('NOAtraum'). Shrub, dp, Noack, 1990. Groundcover with exemplary vigor and disease resistance. Massive clusters on strong arching stems. Grows 24 to 32 inches tall, 4 feet wide. Other colors are now available in this series. 5 to 20 petals. Zones 4 to 11. RIR=7.6

'Frau Dagmar Hartopp'. Hybrid rugosa, mp, Hastrup, 1914. Fragrant single flowers bloom continuously on 4-foot plants. Foliage is rich green and wrinkled. Large crimson hips in fall. 5 petals. Zones 3 to 9. RIR=8.5

Golden Celebration ('AUSgold'). Shrub, dy, Austin, 1993. Blooms up to 5 inches across in clusters on strong, straight stems. Rounded, compact, and medium size, 5 to 6 feet tall. 50+ petals. Zones 4 to 9. RIR=8.0

'Gartendirektor Otto Linne'. Shrub, dp, Lambert, 1934. 30-bloom clusters all summer. Apple green leaves. Disease resistant, vigorous, 6 to 10 feet tall. Train as climber in mild climates. 25 petals. Zones 4 to 9. RIR=8.8

Grootendorst Red ('F.J. Grootendorst'). Hybrid rugosa, mr, de Goey, 1918. Constantly in flower with clusters of 10 to 20 blooms. Very fragrant. 25 petals. 5 feet tall. Zones 3 to 11. RIR=7.8

Gertrude Jekyll ('AUSboard'). Shrub, mp, Austin, 1986. Wonderfully flat blooms with myrrh fragrance. Canes are thorny. Can grow as tall as 10 feet in moderate climates. 50 or more petals. Zones 5 to 10. RIR=7.6

Grootendorst Pink ('Pink Grootendorst'). Hybrid rugosa, mp, Grootendorst, 1923. Masses of small florets with frilled edges. Wrinkled foliage, 6 feet tall. Makes an excellent hedge. 20 petals or more. Zones 4 to 9.

'Hansa'. Hybrid rugosa, mr, Schaum and Van Tol, 1905. Clove fragrance, strong stems. Vigorous and very hardy but sensitive to pesticides. 4 to 5 feet tall. Striking hips. 30 petals. Zones 3 to 9. RIR=8.4

Janet ('AUSpishus'). Shrub, pb, Austin, 2003. Long, arching canes produces lots of flowers with a strong tea fragrance. Can be trained as a climber. 6 to 8 feet tall. 41+ petals. Zones 4 to 11.

Jude the Obscure ('AUSjo'). Shrub, my, Austin, 1995. Large blooms with fruity fragrance reminiscent of guava and sweet white wine. 5 to 7 feet tall. Loves warmth. 55 to 70 petals. Zones 5 to 11. RIR=8.0

Knock Out ('RADrazz'). Shrub, rb, Radler, 1999. This variety's virtual immunity to black spot has set a new standard for landscape roses. 3 to 4 feet tall. 4 to 8 petals. Zones 4 to 11. RIR=8.6
Awards: AARS 2000, PGM 2003

Kaleidoscope ('JACbow'). Shrub, m, Walden, 1999. Unusual, pleasing complementary colors. 3 to 4 feet tall. 35 to 40 petals. Zones 5 to 11. RIR=7.3
Awards: AARS 1999

'Kathleen'. Hybrid musk, lp, Pemberton, 1922. Single-petaled large clusters spring to fall. Golden stamens. Vigorous, 6 to 12 feet tall. Orange hips in fall. 5 petals. Zones 6 to 9. RIR=8.5

Lady Elsie May ('ANGelsie'). Shrub, op, Noack, 2005. Another great addition to worry-free landscape roses, delicately scented. 30 to 35 inches tall and 24 inches wide. 12 to 14 petals. Zones 4 to 11.
Awards: AARS 2005

'Lavender Lassie'. Hybrid musk, m, Kordes, 1960. Large trusses of very fragrant flowers. Pillar growth habit, 8 to 12 feet tall. Foliage is disease resistant. 25 to 30 petals. Zones 4 to 9. RIR=8.2

Leonard Dudley Braithwaite ('AUScrim'). Shrub, dr, Austin, 1988. Wide, slightly cupped flowers bloom continuously all summer. Dark green, disease-resistant foliage. 4 to 6 feet tall. 50+ petals. Zones 6 to 10. RIR=7.9

Linda Campbell ('MORten'). Hybrid rugosa, mr, Moore, 1991. Tall, arching canes 8 to 10 feet tall. Huge sprays; repeat bloomer. Likes heat (ASE and SC). 20 to 25 petals. Zones 4 to 11. RIR=8.1

Mary Rose ('AUSmary'). Shrub, mp, Austin, 1983. Damasklike flowers with ruffled center petals. Vigorous, disease resistant, 4 to 5 feet tall. 50+ petals. Zones 5 to 10. RIR=8.3

'Morden Blush'. Shrub, lp, Collicutt, 1988. Super hardy Parkland rose developed for Canadian climates but also performs well in milder ones. 3 to 5 feet tall. 17 to 25 petals. Zones 4 to 10. RIR=8.0

Othello ('AUSlo'). Shrub, mr, Austin, 1990. Color varies with climate. Use as a large shrub or a low climber, 6 to 7 feet tall. Needs protection from mildew. 50+ petals. Zones 5 to 10. RIR=7.5

Pat Austin ('AUSmum'). Shrub, or, Austin, 1995. Brings an entirely new color to roses with wonderful contrasting coppery tones on the underside of the petals. 4 to 5 feet tall. Zones 5 to 11. RIR=7.7

'Paul's Himalayan Musk Rambler'. Hybrid musk, lp, Paul, 1916. Rosette blooms in large clusters on threadlike stems. Can grow to 30 feet in all directions. Ideal for growing into trees. 17 to 25 petals. Zones 4 to 9. RIR=7.9

Peach Blossom ('AUSblossom'). Shrub, lp, Austin, 1990. Classic soft blush-pink flowers borne in large clusters; slight fragrance. Spreading bushy habit. 6 to 14 petals. Zones 5 to 10. RIR=7.5

Perdita ('AUSperd'). Shrub, ab, Austin, 1983. Blooms change from hybrid tea form to quartered cups and finish as neat rosettes. Needs a season to establish. 4 feet tall. 50+ petals. Zones 5 to 10. RIR=7.8

Peter Beales ('CLEexpert'). Shrub, mr, Clements, 2000. Classic single petals with a strong fragrance. Grows about 4 feet tall and wide. 5 to 8 petals. Zones 5 to 10.

Plum Frost ('JACpluco'). Shrub, m, Walden, 2007. Powerful citrus scent and colorful, large sprays on long stems. Best as a hedge. Hardy. 15 petals. Zones 5 to 10.

'Prosperity'. Hybrid musk, w, Pemberton, 1919. Recurrent, very fragrant. flowers in large clusters. Vigorous. Train as a tall pillar. 20 petals. Zones 6 to 10. RIR=8.5

Rainbow Knock Out ('RADcor'). Shrub, op, Radler, 2007. Latest welcome addition to a series that is clean and carefree; produces an abundance of blooms. Compact and bushy. 5 petals. Zones 5 to 10. AARS 2007

Redouté ('AUSpale'). Shrub, lp, Austin, 1992. Sport of Mary Rose with all its characteristics except color. Good repeat flowering, light fragrance. Medium-size bush, 4 feet tall. 40 to 50 petals. Zones 5 to 10.

Red Ribbons ('KORtemma'). Shrub, mr, Kordes, 1990. Groundcover rose. Hardy, maintenance free, disease resistant. 2 feet tall, 4 feet wide. 20 to 25 petals. Zones 4 to 10. RIR=8.3

Rockin' Robin ('WEKboroco'). Shrub, rb, Carruth, 1997. Has the plant habit of a small fountain covered with blooms. Petite bush of 3 to 4 feet is ideal for small spaces. Mild apple fragrance. 40 to 45 petals. Zones 4 to 11. RIR=7.5

Rosa rugosa. Species, dp. Popular as a thorny, dense hedge. Large red hips in fall. Resistant to salt spray, excellent for seashore. 5 to 7 feet tall. Extremely cold hardy. 5 petals. Zones 2 to 9. RIR=8.9

Rosa rugosa alba. Species, w, prior to 1800. White form of *Rosa rugosa*, with the same cold hardiness, lovely hips, and vigor. 5 petals. Zones 2 to 8. RIR=9.1

'Roseraie de l'Hay'. Hybrid rugosa, dr, Cochet-Cochet, 1901. Large, loose blooms open perfectly flat; repeat blooming with a sugared almond fragrance. Grows 5 to 10 feet tall. 30+ petals. Zones 4 to 9. RIR=8.8

'Sally Holmes'. Shrub, w, Holmes, 1976. Large, long-lasting clusters cover a large spreading bush, 10 feet tall and wide. First spring bloom is best. Makes good pillar. 5 to 8 petals. Zones 5 to 9. RIR=8.9
Awards: PGM 1993

'Sea Foam'. Shrub, w, Schwartz, 1964. Vigorous with very large showy clusters of creamy white flowers with a fresh scent. Often used as groundcover, but can be trained as a climber, pillar, or weeping tree. 2 to 10 feet tall. 35 petals. Zones 4 to 10. RIR=8.2

Simplicity ('JACink' 1978). F, mp, Warriner, 1979. First successful hedge rose. Boasts a profusion of clusters for a dazzling garden display. Plants grow 4 to 5 feet tall. Now available in four colors besides pink: purple, white, yellow, and lavender. 18 petals. Zones 6 to 10. RIR=7.6

St Alban ('AUSchesnut'). Shrub, my, Austin, 2004. An arching shrub loaded with fresh-scent flowers and luxurious foliage. 5 to 6 feet tall. 50+ petals. Zones 5 to 10.

'Sunny June'. Shrub, dy, Lammerts, 1952. Single-petaled, repeated blooms cover polished dark green leaves. Long, lax stems spread wide as a groundcover or can be trained to 8 feet on a trellis. Vigorous. 5 to 7 petals. Zones 5 to 10. RIR=7.8

Symphony ('AUSlett'). Shrub, my, Austin, 1994. Small clusters with light fragrance. Upright growth habit on a smallish bush 4 feet tall. 40 to 50 petals. Zones 5 to 10. RIR=7.8

Tamora ('AUStamora'). Shrub, ab, Austin, 1987. Deeply cupped, long-repeating blooms have a strong myrrh fragrance. Very thorny. Dense, compact, 3 to 4 feet. 40 to 50 petals. Zones 5 to 10. RIR=7.8

The Prince ('AUSvelvet' 1990). Shrub, dr, Austin, 1990. Bloom color deepens with age. Low-growing, spreading bush, 3 feet tall. Substantial fragrance. 100 petals. Zones 5 to 10. RIR=7.7

'Thérèse Bugnet'. Hybrid rugosa, mp, Bugnet, 1950. Bright pink flowers over dark green foliage. Remarkably disease resistant. Can suffer badly from chemical sprays. 4 to 6 feet tall. 35 to 40 petals. Zones 3 to 9. RIR=8.4

Yellow Ribbons ('CHEwpatyel'). Shrub, ly, Walden, 2005. Good groundcover with continual masses of small nonfading blooms that hide the foliage. 18 to 24 inches tall, somewhat wider. 20 to 25 petals. Zones 5 to 10. **Awards:** RHGM 2005

CLIMBERS

A large group of roses produce long, arching canes that can be trained to cover fences, walls, trellises, arbors, and pergolas. This group encompasses all flower sizes and shapes, from miniature florets to large hybrid tea blossoms.

Within climbers are two subdivisions. Roses in the first group—which are the focus of this section—are called "large-flowered climbers." These are true climbers with no bush rose counterparts.

Roses in the second group include the climbing counterparts of already existing varieties, as well as other roses with long canes that are sometimes trained to climb on vertical supports.

Listed below are climbing roses described elsewhere in this gallery. Some are climbing counterparts of hybrid teas, floribundas, and old garden roses. Others are simply roses that have long canes that can be trained to climb:

'Angel Face, Climbing' (F)
Austrian Copper (Species)
Constance Spry (Shrub)
'Dortmund'
Double Delight, Climbing (HT)
'Iceberg, Climbing' (F)
'Jeanne Lajoie' (ClMin)
'Lavender Lassie' (Shrub)
Life Lines (ClMin)
'Marechal Niel' (OGR)
'Mermaid' (OGR)
'Mme Alfred Carriere' (OGR)
'Mme Isaac Pereire' (OGR)
'Old Blush, Climbing' (OGR)
'Peace, Climbing' (HT)
'Playgirl, Climbing' (F)
'Queen Elizabeth, Climbing' Gr)
Rainbow's End, Climbing (ClMin)
Red Cascade (ClMin)
'Reve d'Or' (OGR)
'Sally Holmes' (Shrub)
'Sombreuil' (OGR)
'Souvenir de la Malmaison, Climbing' (OGR)
Sun Flare, Climbing (F)
'Sunsprite, Climbing' (F)
'Zépherine Drouhin' (OGR)

'Aloha'. LCl, mp, Boerner, 1949. Blooms are a delicate rose pink with a darker reverse. A classic variety from the late 1940s with a distinct sweet rose fragrance. 8 to 10 feet. 60+ petals. Zones 7 to 11. RIR=8.0

All Ablaze ('WEKsamsou'). LCl, mr, Carruth, 2000. Large showy clusters of ruffled flowers that give a Christmas effect against the dark green foliage. Hardy, vigorous, and a good repeater, 8 to 10 feet tall. 35+ petals. Best in Zones 5 to 8. RIR=7.4

Altissimo ('DELmur'). LCl, mr, Delbard, 1966. Very large blossoms with golden stamens that spill their pollen onto the petals. Hardy and vigorous, 7 to 15 feet tall. 5 to 7 petals. Zones 6 to 9. RIR=8.5

America ('JACclam' 1976). LCl, op, Warriner, 1976. Blooms are perfectly formed and have a strong spicy fragrance. Late bloomer but repeats well all season. 10 to 12 feet tall. 40 to 45 petals. Zones 6 to 10. RIR=8.3
Awards: AARS 1976

'Autumn Sunset'. LCl, ab, Lowe, 1988. Great hardiness and super disease resistance. Best in cool climates, such as PNW and ANE. 8 to 12 feet tall. 20 to 25 petals. Zones 5 to 10. RIR=8.1

Berries 'n' Cream ('POUlclimb'). LCl, pb, Poulsen, 1998. Covered with large fragrant clusters on strong stems. Disease-free shrub blooms all season. Vigorous, arching 10 to 12 feet high and wide. 25 to 30 petals. Zones 5 to 10. RIR=7.8

'Blaze'. LCl, mr, Kallay, 1932. Great display of large clusters. Consistent performer with good repeat bloom cycle. 12 to 14 feet tall. 20 to 25 petals. Zones 5 to 10. RIR=7.2

Blaze of Glory ('JACamite'). LCl, ob, Jackson & Perkins, 2004. A blossoming dynamo that produces flowers all summer long in giant clusters. Flowers have a light musk fragrance. 12 to 14 feet. 25 petals. Zones 6 to 10.

Brite Eyes ('RADbrite'). LCl, op, Radler, 2006. Perfect for small gardens, this black spot resistant climber offers an amazing salmon color and great fragrance. 6 to 8 feet tall. 7 to 10 petals. Zones 5 to 11.

'Don Juan'. LCl, dr, Malandrone, 1958. Magnificent clusters of shapely blooms throughout the summer. Foliage is glossy and dark green on a vigorous disease-resistant plant. 10 to 12 feet tall. 30 to 35 petals. Zones 6 to 9. RIR=8.2

'Dortmund'. Hybrid kordesii, mr, Kordes, 1955. Medium-size bloom clusters all summer. Vigorous. 10 to 15 feet tall as shrub or a climber. Bright orange hips add fall and winter appeal. Disease resistant and hardy. 5 to 12 petals. Zones 4 to 9. RIR=9.1
Awards: PGM 1971

Dream Weaver ('JACpic'). LCl, op, Zary, 1996. Graceful arching canes provide floribundalike clusters of 3- to 4-inch bright coral-pink flowers. Light old rose fragrance. 10 to 12 feet. 30 petals. Zones 4 to 11. RIR=7.9

Dublin Bay ('MACdub'). LCl, mr, McGredy, 1975. Lots of blooms in small sprays. Train as a pillar or a climber. Well suited to cooler (ANE) and warmer (ASE) climates. 8 to 10 feet tall. 25 petals. Zones 4 to 11. RIR=8.6

Eden ('MEIviolin'). LCl, pb, Meilland, 1987. Also sold as 'Pierre de Ronsard'. Blooms in small clusters on vigorous disease-resistant bush. Ideal for lampposts and gazebos. 10 to 12 feet tall. Lightly fragrant. 40+ petals. Zones 4 to 9. RIR=8.2
Awards: WFRS/HOF 2006

Fourth of July ('WEKroalt'). LCl, rb, Carruth, 1999. Super vigorous climber provides big sprays of long-lasting striped blooms with apple-and-rose fragrance. 10 to 14 feet tall. 10 to 15 petals. Zones 5 to 11. RIR=8.1
Awards: AARS 1999, RHGM 2002

'Golden Showers'. LCl, my, Lammerts, 1956. AARS. Small clusters on a vigorous climber. Licorice fragrance. Best in cool climates, such as PNW and ANE. 10 to 12 feet tall. 25 to 28 petals. Zones 6 to 9. RIR=7.4
Awards: AARS 1957, PGM 1957

Handel ('MACha'). LCl, rb, McGredy, 1965. Blooms come one to a stem or in small sprays. Best in cool climates, such as ANE and PNW. 10 to 12 feet tall. 20 to 30 petals. Zones 5 to 9. RIR=7.9
Awards: PGM 1975

'Henry Kelsey'. Hybrid kordesii, mr, Svejda, 1984. Semidouble dark red flowers with bright yellow stamens all summer. Spicy fragrance. 8 to 10 feet tall, glossy dark green leaves. One of the hardiest climbers. Zones 3 to 9.

High Hopes ('HARyup'). LCl, mp, Harkness, 1994. Clusters of 3 or 4 blooms with a spicy scent. Prefers to grow upright as a pillar. 10 to 12 feet tall. 32 petals. Zones 5 to 11.

High Society ('JACadyna'). LCl, dp, Zary, 2004. Large classically shaped blooms adorn this vigorous, high-spirited rose with a light damask fragrance. 30 to 35 petals. Zones 5 to 10.

'Joseph's Coat'. LCl, rb, Armstrong & Swim, 1964. Popular variety because of its multitoned color display. Produces lots of big clusters throughout the growing season. 10 to 12 feet tall. 23 to 28 petals. Zones 4 to 10. RIR=7.5

Lace Casade ('JACarch'). LCl, w, Warriner, 1992. Noted for exhibiting fountains of white blooms in small clusters on long, arching canes. 6 to 7 feet tall. 20 petals. Zones 5 to 11. RIR=7.9

'Mlle Cécile Brünner, Climbing'. CLPol, lp, 1894. Large sprays cover the plant. Grows 20 to 30 feet in all directions; can cover a house or climb a tree. 30+ petals. Zones 6 to 10. RIR=8.4
Awards: WFRS/OGR

'New Dawn'. LCl, lp, Somerset, 1930. Fragrant flowers appear all season. Extremely vigorous and hardy. Grows well in nearly all climates. 18 to 20 feet tall. 35 to 40 petals. Zones 4 to 10. RIR=8.6
Awards: WFRS/HOF 1997

'Newport Fairy'. Rambler, pb, Gardner, 1908. This hybrid wichurana bears small blooms in enormous clusters. Sprawls 20 to 30 feet in all directions. Spring bloom is spectacular; repeat can be slow in cool climates. 5 petals. Zones 5 to 10. RIR=8.5

Night Owl ('WEKpurosot'). LCl, m, Carruth, 2006. What a color! Clusters with showy, sweetly fragrant flowers that are both long lived and nonfading. 10 to 14 feet tall. 8 to 10 petals. Zones 5 to 11.

Paprika ('MEIriental'). LCl, or, Meilland, 1997. Semidouble flowers are bright orange-red. Light fragrance. Dense foliage is dark green. 8 to 10 feet tall. Zones 5 to 10.

Pearly Gates ('WEKmeyer'). LCl, lp, Meyer, 1999. Huge, well-formed flowers ooze with a strong spicy fragrance. Slow to bloom in spring. 10 to 12 feet tall. 35 petals. Zones 6 to 10. RIR=7.7

***Rosa banksia lutea* (Yellow Lady Banks Rose).** Species, ly, 1824. Abundant clusters of small, double flowers produced once in spring. Can grow up to 30 feet in all directions, with trunks the size of small trees. Excellent on high walls or in mature trees where support is sturdy. 17 to 25 petals. Zones 7 to 10. RIR=9.1

'Royal Sunset'. LCl, ab, Morey, 1960. Abundant, large blooms all summer. Glossy, dark foliage. Best in cool climates, such as PWN and ANE. Vigorous, 8 to 10 feet tall. Moderate fragrance. 20 to 25 petals. Zones 6 to 10. RIR=8.9 **Awards:** PGM 1960

Scent from Above ('CHEwgoldtop'). LCl, my, Warner, 2005. Elegant blooms that keep their color in strong sunlight. 3 to 4 inches across, with a licorice scent. 8 to 10 feet. Zones 5-10.

Sky's The Limit ('WEKprimsoul'). LCl, my, Carruth, 2007. Clusters of blooms cover the bush from top to bottom. Hardy and vigorous. 10 to 12 feet. 20to 25 petals. Zones 5 to 10.

Soaring Spirits ('WEKbecfoj'). LCl, pb, Carruth, 2005. Named to honor the victims of 9/11, blooms are showy and attractive in the garden. Scent is of fresh-cut apple. 8 to 12 feet tall. 5 to 8 petals. Zones 5 to 10.

Social Climber ('JACweave'). LCl, dp, Jackson & Perkins, 2004. One of the few full-petaled varieties with a classical form. Blooms are large, 3 to 4 inch diameter. 6 feet tall. 40 petals. Zones 5 to 10.

Stairway to Heaven ('JACetima'). LCl, mr, Jackson & Perkins, 2002. Has a rambling characteristic with very strong, healthy lateral canes that yield an abundance of spicy-scented clusters. 10 to 12 feet tall. 25 petals. Zones 5 to 11. RIR=7.3

Summer Wine ('KORizont'). LCl, dp, Kordes, 1985. Large coral-pink flowers with attractive contrasting stamens have only a slight fragrance. 8 to 10 feet tall. 5 petals. Zones 5 to 11.

Westerland ('KORwest'). Shrub, ab, Kordes, 1970. Terrific fragrance, and large long-lasting clusters of flowers on a hardy vigorous plant. 10 to 12 feet tall. 18 to 25 petals. RIR=8.2

'White Dawn'. LCl, w, Longley, 1949. Proven performer displays weatherproof ruffled blooms spring to fall. Vigorous and disease free, 10 to 12 feet tall. Performs well in all climates. 30 to 35 petals. Zones 6 to 9. RIR=7.7

'William Baffin'. Hybrid kordesii, dp, Svejda, 1983. Extremely cold hardy. Florets in clusters of up to 30 blooms per stem from summer to fall. Glossy, disease-resistant foliage. 10 to 12 feet tall. 20 petals. Zones 3 to 9. RIR=8.9.

ROSE RESOURCES

▲ **The headquarters of the American Rose Society in Shreveport, Louisiana.**

American Rose Society (ARS)

Gardeners who enjoy growing roses often need some help as well as a way to share their experiences. The American Rose Society (ARS) is a national nonprofit organization composed of a network of about 300 local rose societies located in 10 major geographical regions throughout the United States. Headquartered in Shreveport, Louisiana, the ARS maintains a 118-acre park known as the American Rose Center, which is dedicated to roses. With more than 16,000 members, the ARS offers the following services to promote rose growing:

■ Provides access to more than 3,000 Consulting Rosarians who offer personal rose-growing assistance. There's one in your area who can answer your questions.

■ Lists affiliated rose societies in your area, where you can learn even more about rose growing and make new friends.

■ Publishes an annual *Handbook for Selecting Roses*, which contains Roses in Review ratings.

■ Publishes a full-color monthly magazine, *The American Rose,* devoted to cultural information, tips, and advice.

■ Publishes the *American Rose Annual,* a full-color volume containing the latest information on roses and rose culture.

■ Publishes four quarterly publications dealing with specialized subjects: *Miniature Roses, Old Garden Roses, Rose Arrangements,* and *Rose Exhibiting.*

■ Maintains a lending library of books, videos, and slide series that can be borrowed through the mail.

■ Holds annual conventions and rose shows featuring lectures, garden tours, and a chance to meet with fellow rose growers from all over the nation.

The ARS website (www.ars.org) offers features such as "Rose of the Month," articles by experts on selected topics, links to local rose societies, answers to frequently asked questions, where to buy roses, and much more. This site is updated regularly.

Joining the ARS is certainly a step to becoming a better rose grower. The benefits of membership can lead you to expanding your garden, gaining new friendships, and most of all, improving your rose-growing techniques. For more information, call 800-637-6534 or write to: American Rose Society, P.O. Box 30,000, Shreveport, LA 71130.

The World Federation of Rose Societies (WFRS)

The objectives of the World Federation of Rose Societies, founded in 1968, are to encourage and facilitate the interchange of information about and knowledge of the rose among national rose societies; to coordinate international conventions and exhibitions; to encourage and sponsor research into problems concerning the rose; to establish common standards for judging new rose seedlings; to establish a uniform system of rose classification; to grant international honors and awards; and to encourage and advance international corporation on all other matters concerning the rose.

The World Federation of Rose Societies website (www.worldrose.org) provides a global perspective on roses and also features the prize-winning varieties voted into the Rose Hall of Fame. The site lists coming events, including worldwide conferences and conventions, and includes editorials from the organization's twice-yearly newsletter, *World Rose News.* It also includes links to national rose societies.

Exploring the Internet

The following organizations have web pages full of photos and information on roses and rose growing.

■ All-America Rose Selections (www.rose.org) provides lists and photographs of award winners from 1940 to the present. The website also has a search feature that allows visitors to access a list of prominent rose gardens by state.

■ Royal National Rose Society (www.rnrs.org) offers the benefits of membership plus insight into rose gardens in the United Kingdom, care information, events, publications, and more.

■ Canadian Rose Society (www.canadianrosesociety. org) lists current events and shows, public gardens, instructions on how to plant and select roses.

■ HelpMeFind/Roses (www. helpmefind.com/roses) lists, describes, and provides photographs and sources for more than 28,000 varieties and species of roses.

INDEX

Note: Page references in **bold type** indicate gallery entries. Page references in *italic type indicate additional photographs, illustrations, or information in captions.*

ROSE INDEX

SUBJECT INDEX

METRIC CONVERSIONS

U.S. UNITS TO METRIC EQUIVALENTS			METRIC EQUIVALENTS TO U.S. UNITS		
To Convert From	Multiply by	To Get	To Convert From	Multiply by	To Get
Inches	25.4	Millimeters	Millimeters	0.0394	Inches
Inches	2.54	Centimeters	Centimeters	0.3937	Inches
Feet	30.48	Centimeters	Centimeters	0.0328	Feet
Feet	0.3048	Meters	Meters	3.2808	Feet
Yards	0.9144	Meters	Meters	1.0936	Yards

To convert from degrees Fahrenheit (F) to degrees Celsius (C), first subtract 32, then multiply by ⅝.

To convert from degrees Celsius to degrees Fahrenheit, multiply by ⅝, then add 32.

BEAUTIFY YOUR YARD with Scotts® and Miracle-Gro®

Pick up these exciting titles from the brands you trust for gardening expertise—wherever gardening books are sold.